TOUJOURS
LA FRANCE!

TOUJOURS LA FRANCE!

Living the Dream in Rural France

Janine Marsh

Michael O'Mara Books Limited
First published in Great Britain in 2022 by
Michael O'Mara Books Limited
9 Lion Yard
Tremadoc Road
London SW4 7NQ

A CIP catalogue record for this book is available from the British
Library.

Papers used by Michael O'Mara Books Limited are natural, recyclable
products made from wood grown in sustainable forests. The
manufacturing processes conform to the environmental regulations of
the country of origin.

ISBN: 978-1-78929-384-5 in paperback print format
ISBN: 978-1-78929-385-2 in ebook format

1 2 3 4 5 6 7 8 9 10

Typeset by Claire Cater
Cover illustration by Emma Block
Cover design by Ana Bjezancevic and Natasha Le Coultre

Printed and bound by CPI Group (UK) Ltd, Croydon, CR0 4YY

www.mombooks.com

Contents

For my mum, who would have so loved my French life and who inspires me every day to live and love.

Prologue

I OFTEN FEEL that our life in France is largely due to sheer good luck. I met Mark in 1998. I was divorced with a young son, Harry, and a mortgage to pay. I'd been without a car for several years as I simply couldn't afford one; Harry and I went everywhere by bike or bus and we carried our shopping home from the supermarket in a rucksack. When a friend told me that they knew someone who owned a garage and who was selling a very cheap car that might be just right for me, I bought it without even seeing it. The friend of the friend delivered it to my house while I was at work. I came home to find a decrepit, dented and definitely-not-working vehicle. The boot was jammed shut and when I turned the key in the ignition, the disappointing sound of silence followed.

'Aha,' said the car seller when I phoned to complain. 'It likely just needs a tune-up.'

I looked through the free local newspaper for adverts offering mobile mechanic services, since there was clearly no way I could drive the car to a garage. The first number I called was answered by a woman who told me that her brother could fit the car in for a service at my house the following Saturday.

The defunct vehicle never did start and I had to pay to have it towed away. But instead of gaining a working car, I got the mechanic, Mark. We hit it off from the moment our eyes first met. He looked at the car, said it was a pile of crap, came in for a cup of tea and we ended up talking into the next morning. He too was divorced, and had four children. We were born in the same hospital in inner London, albeit two years apart, and we'd lived in the same London suburb as children. Mark was also a frequent visitor to the branch of McDonald's where I'd worked as a teenager during my college days. The more we talked, the more we discovered the many ways that our paths had crossed in the past. We felt as if we had been destined to meet. Mark never left. Three years later, we got married.

It was also fate that led us to France. On a day trip to Calais in 2004 to buy wine with my widowed dad (my mum had died two years before), we looked at three bargain-basement houses on a whim and I fell in love with a dilapidated old farmhouse. We bought it as a holiday home for less than the cost of a posh handbag. Several years later, it was Mark who pushed me out of my comfort zone by suggesting that we took the risk of giving up our jobs in the UK to try to make a new life in France.

It's been a long journey to get to this point and it's an ongoing journey to make it the life we dreamed of …

Janine Marsh

CHAPTER 1

The life and soul
of the party

AFTER A LONG, wet spring that had persistently soaked the Seven Valleys, the sun had at last arrived and it seemed as though it might be willing to stay for a while. But though Jean-Claude was certain, the look of concern on the faces of those who sat around the small wooden table in his kitchen was evident.

'You're quite sure it will be sunny on Saturday?' asked Petit Frère (nicknamed 'Little Brother' despite being in his mid-fifties, as he was the youngest of ten siblings), mopping his forehead with a tissue. It was horribly hot in the small room. A huge wood fire had been lit under Jean-Claude's supersized chimney, despite the sun's rays pouring in through the window.

'It's definitely going to be really sunny and really warm,' Jean-Claude confidently predicted.

At this declaration, everyone looked very gloomy

indeed. Our favourite neighbour was more often wrong than right about the weather, and most of us who knew him well would bet on the exact opposite of whatever he prophesied. Perhaps, like me, everyone was remembering the events of the year before, when Jean-Claude had organized a barbecue to celebrate his wedding anniversary, or 'thirty-five years of being nagged' as he had called it behind his wife's back. His prediction of blue skies on that particular day had been based on ant activity in his garden: 'They've been slow-moving all day,' he said. 'It means no rain. They move faster before the clouds open, making sure their dens are protected.' He couldn't have been more wrong. We had ended up spending the entire time huddled in the garage attached to the side of his house, watching the torrential rain create a river that hurtled down the hill outside the property, while getting headaches from the relentless rumble of his ancient boiler, which was so loud that we all had to shout to hear each other over the din.

In the kitchen, Bernadette, Jean-Claude's wife, handed each of us a tall glass. Petit Frère, Mark, me, Madame Bernadette (we all call her that because there are three Bernadettes in the village – the third is known as Old Madame Bernadette), Constance, Madame Rohart and Claude-who-lives-at-the-top-of-the-hill (father of Claude-who-lives-at-the-bottom-of-the-hill) were members of a small committee with just one job, and a sunny day would most certainly help to make the event that we were organizing more successful.

'*Bah*, for once he may be right,' said Bernadette, in an attempt to reassure everyone. 'Météo forecasts sun all weekend.' Although never that reliable either, the official French weather forecaster was definitely more of a sure thing than Jean-Claude.

She placed a bowl of ice on the table together with a yellow plastic jug containing water and a bottle of pastis. This was the final committee meeting and we would celebrate with a traditional drink. There wasn't enough room for us all to be sitting down, so I was perched on Mark's lap and around the rest of the table sat Madame Bernadette, who was petite and white-haired, Madame Rohart, with a small ginger kitten on her ample lap whose mother was watching from under the table, and Constance, one of the best cooks in the village. The others stood. Petit Frère was closest to the fire and his face had turned almost as red as his russet-coloured hair. Claude was standing next to the sink with Jean-Claude, where Bernadette could keep a watchful eye on them and make sure they didn't sneak off to talk about pigeons or pumpkins, their two favourite things.

For several weeks we had met once a week in this little kitchen to arrange a party for Claudette, Bernadette's mother, whose eighty-sixth birthday was imminent. Under the watchful eye of Jean-Claude's great-grandfather Albert, whose photo sat proudly on top of

11

a dresser packed with cups, jugs, glasses and miniature figurines, we had plotted, planned and prepared for the big day.

Almost all of Jean-Claude's proposals had been rejected as he had a tendency to get carried away. His outlandish suggestions had included: laying a red carpet into the *salle des fêtes* where the party would be held, as it was due to take place just before the Cannes Film Festival; having fire-eaters for entertainment; and everyone dressing up as members of the British royal family because Claudette is a huge fan.

'*Non, non* and *non*,' said Bernadette sternly. 'This is a secret party. Maman knows nothing about it and I want it kept that way. I want no rumours of red carpets and talk of dressing up like a queen getting back to her.'

The food had been decided, the wine, beer and aperitifs chosen, the guest list agreed. Each of us had been allocated different jobs. Now all we had to do was carry out our roles to Bernadette's satisfaction and make the day special for Claudette. The celebratory bottle of pastis was passed around the room, with everyone adding water to their measures and then ice, turning the pastis a milky-soft yellow, the aroma of aniseed filling the air. 'Ah, *le petit jaune*, the little yellow one, how I've missed you,' said Jean-Claude reverentially, as he enthusiastically stuck his nose into the glass and sniffed deeply.

Pastis is hugely popular in France, and is as much a national drink as wine. It's drunk neat or with water, which turns it cloudy and makes it thankfully less potent. Drink too much pastis and you're likely to turn cloudy yourself, as it contains a whopping 40 to 45 per cent alcohol. There's even a saying in French: '*Je suis dans le pastis*', which means 'I am in trouble'. Rather an appropriate phrase for what came next.

Bernadette had given each of us a sheet of paper detailing our jobs. Constance, Madame Bernadette and Madame Rohart would be baking with Bernadette over the next few days. There were also a few non-committee members involved in making the food. I was to go and collect the cheese from Fromagerie Caseus in Montreuil-sur-Mer, which, as everyone around here knows, is one of the best cheese shops in the north. Then I was to help where needed with the cooking and make sure that Bread Man delivered the baguettes, bread, quiches and pies on time. The men were to ensure that the tables and chairs were all set out on the day, blow up balloons and organize the DJ. A local wine merchant was delivering the wine, beer and liqueurs together with glasses.

'There will be sixty people coming to the party,' announced Bernadette, looking at the list we'd drawn up.

'Ahem!' Jean-Claude cleared his throat. Bernadette's head swivelled in his direction. 'When I was at the *pharmacie* the other day, I saw Audrey and Enzo and they said to give their love to Claudette, so I said, "Why don't you give it to her yourself? We're having a party on

Saturday at midday in the *salle des fêtes* …"' Jean-Claude took a nervous slurp of his pastis.

'Right. There will be sixty-two people coming to the party,' said Bernadette.

'Ah, Baptiste the plumber and his friend Antoine were there too, and they heard me talking to Audrey and Enzo. They asked if they could come and I couldn't really say no …' Another slurp.

'Sixty-four people it is then,' replied Bernadette, looking a little annoyed now.

'Maybe they will bring their wives with them,' suggested Jean-Claude hastily, tipping more pastis into his glass as Bernadette frowned at him.

'Um …' piped up Madame Bernadette. She faltered a little as Bernadette turned her beady eyes towards her. 'I, ah, saw Sister Maria at the market in Beaurainville last week and we were chatting about the good old days, and she asked after Claudette and I mentioned the party, and she said how much she'd love to come and I said I was sure you wouldn't mind …' Her voice trailed off and she too took a sip of pastis.

We all did.

Bernadette looked at me. 'Have you invited anyone else?' she asked.

'No, I haven't.'

'Mark – have you invited anyone else?'

'No,' he replied, keeping his eyes firmly on the pastis in his hand.

'The only *Anglais* in the village have behaved. What about the French? Has anyone else invited anyone and forgotten to tell me?' Bernadette is a small woman but has plenty of presence, and we were all feeling the force of it as she looked slowly round the room.

'Sister Maria said that Sister Catherine would love to come too,' Madame Bernadette admitted quickly.

Petit Frère shook his head vigorously, '*Non*, not me,' he said, not daring to look at Jean-Claude.

'Me neither,' declared Constance as Bernadette's narrowed eyes turned her way, and Madame Rohart hurriedly agreed that she had not done anything to irk Bernadette.

'Right. I need to adjust the shopping requirements. Give me back your lists. Jean-Claude will deliver them to you this afternoon.' He was unusually quiet in his corner but smiled sweetly at his wife – he knew she would eventually forgive him once she'd had a bit of a moan.

It was almost noon and we knew better than to outstay our welcome: the two-hour lunch break is something that is still firmly upheld in these parts. Mark and I walked the short distance through the village to our home, gaining a canine round of applause in the form of wild barking from our dogs Ella Fitzgerald, Churchill and Frank Bruno (more commonly known as 'Bruno') when we pushed open the squeaky gate. Three of our eight cats were lolling on the table in the front garden, sunning themselves and generally making it clear that they were in charge, not us.

It sometimes feels as if we live in an animal sanctuary. In our BF (Before France) lives, we had lived in a semi-detached house in suburban London and the closest we got to an animal was when one of the kids brought a rat home from the school laboratory to look after during the holidays. Within months of moving to France, we acquired Winston the cat after we found him, as a month-old kitten, being attacked by a larger cat under a wheel of our van in the town of Boulogne-sur-Mer on the Opal Coast. Churchill the German pinscher rapidly followed, as we were told he was going to be put down if no one bought him from the pet shop where he was living in a glass cage. Weeks later, Ella Fitzgerald arrived. Supposedly a type of spaniel, she turned out to be a German shepherd cross and had also lived with Churchill in the cage. We were told that she too was due to be euthanized (sometimes, I think they saw us coming). A kitten appeared at the back door one day and refused to leave – we called him 'Enry Cooper. Frank Bruno, an abandoned Labrador, also moved in. A clowder of stray cats followed – Ginger Roger (deaf), Hank Marvin He's Always Starvin' (one-eyed), Loulou (princess), Shadow (nervy), Fat Cat (lives up to his name), Little Socks (black cat, white feet), Ugly Cat (no tail and a squashed face) and Marie-Antoinette. Before we knew it, a pack of dogs and a hoard of tiny tigers were prowling round the house, demanding attention, clawing at everything and clamouring for treats.

We heard a hooter being sounded nearby – Bread Man was on the way, so we stepped back into the road to await him.

Here in the Seven Valleys, in the northern tip of France, many little hamlets and villages are dotted among the hills, nestled alongside streams and perched on the edge of forests, and many have no shops, so basic food is delivered to individual homes – bread, fish, meat, dairy and groceries. Three times a week, come rain, sun or snow, Bread Man drives his little van from village to village, stopping outside houses to pop baguettes into long thin bags left on gate hooks or hung from windows. He also drops off freshly baked *boulots* (crusty, round country loaves), many types of bread, croissants, cakes and pastries. He's a lifeline for older villagers who don't drive and saves all of us from having to get in our cars to go to a boulangerie: eco-friendly long before it became fashionable.

Before Bread Man reaches our house, he stops at Claudette's next door and presses the van's horn for several seconds – as she's a little hard of hearing – to summon her to collect her bread. Seeing us waiting in the road, she took her loaf and beckoned us up the hill.

Small in stature and slim, she was wearing her pink rubber boots and a floral pinafore over her navy dress, her snowy white hair tied back. She once told me that she has never in her whole life worn a pair of trousers. I asked her if it was because until 2013 it was technically illegal for women to wear trousers in France – which is actually true, though not enforced in many years. The law was introduced in November 1800 to prevent women from doing certain jobs, and was amended a hundred years or so later to allow women to don a pair of trousers if they were riding a horse or a bike. 'No,' laughed Claudette, 'it's because I like to wear dresses.' The late great French designer Yves Saint Laurent once said that what is important in a dress is the woman who's wearing it – I reckon he would have loved Claudette …

'Your cockerel is in my back garden. Do you want to come and get him?'

It was the second time that week that we'd been summoned by Claudette to capture the renegade bird. Taking our baguette and saying goodbye to Bread Man, we followed her across the courtyard, wiped our feet on the tea towel spread on the doorstep of her house (she is very house-proud), walked through the kitchen and into the garden. We heard the bird before we saw him, crowing for all he was worth. Claudette strode up to him and grabbed him firmly by the neck. Shocked, he choked back a cock-a-doodle-doo, presumably never expecting such a sweet old lady to move so quickly, and was unceremoniously thrust towards us.

'What do you call this one?' she asked, after she'd released him back into our care.

My neighbours find it strange that I give names to my birds. They hear me in the garden calling out 'Brad Pitt, pack that up', 'Joan Crawford, stop pecking Sophia Loren' and such like. When we first came to France, we were determined to live a more sustainable lifestyle – grow our own vegetables and fruit, keep animals for eggs and meat. The very first time that we were confronted with the reality of eating one of our cockerels, though, we realized that it was a doomed dream. Eaglet was our first cockerel and when he fell out of the coop and broke a leg, we had no choice but to put him out of his misery. Then we turned him into coq au vin. It smelled mouth-wateringly wonderful. It looked lip-smackingly scrumptious. But we couldn't eat him. We turned to each other and put our knives and forks down. Jean-Claude had told us from the very start not to name our animals: 'You'll struggle if you do. They will be pets, not pot fodder.' He was right, of course. Now we hardly touch meat and wouldn't dream of eating our birds – we have sixty feathered pets instead!

'That one,' I said, 'is George Clooney.'

'*Bah*, I can't see the likeness, but he has a good strong voice. You should call him Serge Gainsbourg. Stick him in this box to take him home, and come and talk to me.'

We took off our boots and sat at the wooden table in the always-warm kitchen, thanks to the coal and wood oven that's more than sixty years old and is constantly lit for the hot-water supply as well as for cooking. Claudette bent to retrieve three tiny glasses from an antique dark-wood sideboard, its top covered in lacy doilies, a wooden crucifix, a mix of black-and-white and colour family photos, and a white jug filled with pink roses and wild flowers. From the fridge, on top of which sits an ancient TV, she took a dark-green glass bottle, gave it a swirl and pulled out the stopper, causing a satisfying 'pop'.

'Last year's *vin de noix* – it's a particularly good one from the tree in Bernadette's garden,' she said, smiling.

Every June, it's a tradition here to collect green walnuts and pickle them in a mixture of wine and strong alcohol, such as vodka or brandy, together with a large dollop of sugar. I knew I wouldn't get much work done that afternoon.

'It's my birthday at the weekend,' Claudette said, as she poured a tiny drop into each glass, 'and I probably won't see you as I think Bernadette is coming to take me out for the day – she doesn't know that I know, so don't tell her – instead, we can say a toast to me now.'

I tried not to smile, which was easy when I held the potion to my lips, as the fumes stung my eyes; it's horribly potent stuff, liable to strip off the fur from your tongue. In the corner, George Clooney was trying to escape, scratching at the sides of the box, jumping about and making it rock, and filling the kitchen with his loud, angry screeches.

'Be quiet,' said Claudette firmly, placing a cloth over the box. As if by magic, the cockerel stopped its rumpus and the kitchen was once again silent, except for the ticking of a large, square, gold-coloured, 1960s-era clock on the wall.

Claudette was born in this house and has lived here all her life. Even when she married, she occupied the upstairs rooms while her parents lived downstairs. She loves to talk about her husband who passed away long ago, but who is never far from her memory.

'At this time of the year he'd be out in the fields and we would have had lambs to look after. Sometimes the hay would be ready to cut by late spring, and there were constant repairs made to the barns and outbuildings. It was always busy – life is tough for farmers, that never changes. He always came home for lunch and I would cook for him. *Mon Dieu*, he knew how to eat, that one. I miss him still so much. But I am lucky, I never feel alone with my family and friends so close by. Jean-Claude comes every day for lunch and he is an even better eater than my man was.'

In the nine decades since Claudette was born, much in the village has changed and yet nothing seems different. Nature is, as it always was, everything for those who work the land; a constant gift and sometimes a challenge.

We chatted for an hour, and when we left Claudette reminded us not to let on to Bernadette that she knew she was being taken out for her birthday.

We wished Claudette a *bon anniversaire* for the weekend and departed with the peeved cockerel, whom we returned to the pen after clipping his wing feathers in an attempt to stop him from escaping again.

Jean-Claude popped by in the afternoon with our updated job sheets. He's known to all in these parts as Monsieur Partout, 'Mr Everywhere', because wherever you go, he seems to pop up – but the real reason for his wandering is to keep out of Bernadette's way.

'Coffee? *Non*, I need something stronger than that. *Zut*, my wife does my head in sometimes, she breaks my *bonbons*.' (The polite translation of *bonbons* used in this context is 'sweets'.)

It's true that Bernadette likes things to be done properly and that pretty much everyone calls her Le Chef (The Chief), though not to her face. She is obsessed with housework and now, newly retired, she is very firmly in charge of things at home. Jean-Claude, who hasn't worked for years because of his heart condition – which as far as I can tell has never stopped him from enjoying himself – has been roped in to help keep the house clean, the hedges cut, the lawn mowed; even the external walls of the house are regularly dusted. And when Bernadette isn't tidying her own house, she's at her mother's house, cleaning there. Jean-Claude has become very adept at finding things to do elsewhere, which often involves him coming to our house to tell us important news (or, as Mark calls it, skiving). The day before, he had dropped by to let us know that the mayor was definitely going ahead with his plans to automate the village church bells. No more bell-ringing by hand – a machine would do it all from now on. It was the topic of much discussion. Half of the people in the village were in favour of progress and half were against. Jean-Claude was in the latter camp, asking the question: if we no longer teach the local children to ring the bells, what will happen if the machine breaks?

'If you put all your eggs in one basket, you'll have to watch that basket like a hawk,' he said.

'Or get the machine mended,' the mayor had replied, drily.

'What do you think of the new *stade*?' I asked Jean-Claude.

His nose lifted from his glass of red wine, his eyes narrowed and he thumped the table, waking Winston the cat who had been snoring in his basket in the corner.

The mayor, who is young and a go-getter, a man who loves to run marathons for fun, was having a football stadium built for the local kids. This, coming after street lamps, a pavement and vast tubs of flowers, as well as three pedestrian crossings and a speed bump – in a village of 142 people, where passing cars are so rare that they cause the inhabitants to look up – had made us the talk of the valleys. There was even the possibility of a leap into the twenty-first century with rumours of a mobile-phone signal being organized (mind you, that has been talked about for a decade) and the arrival of high-speed internet.

'Ah, the "Stade de France",' Jean-Claude chuckled. 'I used to play football myself, you know.'

It was hard to imagine that he had ever run after anything, let alone a ball. He is a man who loves the finer things in life, and this is reflected in his cake, cheese and wine-loving frame. He often says that although he is not rich, some things – by which he means of an edible nature – are worth spending good money on. He only buys from artisans and local producers, and barters eggs, fruit and vegetables from his enormous garden as much as possible. I told him that Oscar Wilde once wrote that some people know the price of everything and the value of nothing – he now claims these as his own wise words. If anyone dares to say that he could have got something cheaper in the supermarket, he furrows his bushy eyebrows and quotes Wilde in his best French, which takes a bit of doing as he has a very strong local accent.

Like most people in these parts, Jean-Claude speaks a local patois known as Ch'ti. The words are not the same as pure French; many terms for common things are different, for example, 'car' in French is *voiture* but in Ch'ti it's *ch'carette*, *fou* (fool) is *babache* and *je t'aime* (I love you) is *j'viens t'ker*. And there are expressions that make no sense to non-locals. The word *quoi*, for instance, which means 'what' in French, doesn't mean 'what' in Ch'ti but is more like 'erm', which can make following a sentence very difficult. And French words

24

with an 's' sound that begin with 'c' or 'ç' are spelled with a 'ch' in Ch'ti, so *ça va* becomes *cha va* (pronounced 'sha va'). And Jean-Claude is not a *gourmand* but a *goulaf*. If you're having trouble keeping up with this, imagine how we felt when we first arrived, having attempted to learn French only to discover that the natives spoke something completely different!

Sometimes when I sit and talk to some of my elderly neighbours, and Jean-Claude, I have to concentrate really hard to understand what they are saying. Despite having had a home in France for fifteen years, and keeping a Ch'ti dictionary to hand, I've not mastered the art of speaking like the locals, though I apparently also now have a Ch'ti accent. My friends from the south of France tell me they can tell I'm from the north when I speak French, and I'm very proud of that.

'I nearly forgot … Bernadette told me to give you this,' Jean-Claude said, handing us a pot with a flowering lily of the valley, 'because you were out when she brought it up for you last week.'

The first of May is *La Fête du muguet* in France. *Muguet* means 'lily of the valley', and for almost 500 years it's been a tradition to give these delicate, pretty flowers to those whom you love. It all began in 1561 when King Charles IX of France was given a sprig on 1 May and he thought it such a lovely idea that he gave lily of the valley flowers to all the ladies of the court for May Day the following year, and the habit became part of French history. It feels like acceptance when our friends include us too.

Much as I love lily of the valley, I don't have any in my garden because it's highly poisonous and my chickens, despite my best efforts to enclose them, are like feathered Houdinis. They have large pens, plenty of toys to keep them stimulated, the maid (me) turns up with food on time, cleans up after them and generally spoils them. I even play them music sometimes – they love Lady Gaga and Johnny Cash. But still the grass is greener and several of them frequently escape, with Mae West and Zsa Zsa Gabor in particular being fond of scaling the fence and helping themselves to whatever takes their fancy. Baby lettuces? Oh yes. Rose petals, magnolia blooms and any vegetables at all are irresistible to this pair, so I don't take any chances with lily of the valley. The plant looked lovely on the kitchen table, though, and filled the room with its sweet scent.

Jean-Claude looked at his watch and stood up – he had strict instructions from Bernadette to make sure everyone was given their job lists and he couldn't sit chatting all day, he told us.

The rest of the week went by in a whirlwind of preparations for the party. Constance, Madame Rohart, Madame Bernadette and Bernadette baked cakes, made tapenade from black and green olives and cooked delicate little tarts filled with smoked salmon and diced chicken in a creamy sauce. They marinated mushrooms in olive oil flavoured with truffles and prepared potato salad and *le potjevleesch*, one of Madame Bernadette's specialities. This regional dish is not to everyone's taste: it's made from four different meats (rabbit, chicken, pork and veal) marinated in dark beer with herbs, lemon and vegetables, and preserved in jelly – a vegetarian's nightmare. It's Flemish in origin and Madame Bernadette told me that the recipe differs in every home. Hers had been passed down through generations of her family going back at least 200 years, though the dish itself was first made in medieval times. It's so popular in these parts that there is even a contest for the best *pot'je*, as it's lovingly called. In Madame Bernadette's tiny kitchen, we had chopped, peeled and boiled for a whole afternoon and then put the mix into glass jars – all the better to admire the lumpy jellified concoction, which is served cold with chips. Sometimes when I think that I am becoming almost French, I remember attempting to eat *potjevleesch* when we first came here – it's something I know that I will never try again – and I realize that I am not quite there yet.

Eventually, the big day arrived and there was still a lot to do before the party kicked off at noon. We were up with the lark – quite literally. It was a perfect May morning as Mark and I sat and drank tea in the garden while the sun rose slowly into a cloudless, bright, powder-blue sky over a largely silent little village. A far cry from the noises we were used to BF (Before

France) – police sirens, aeroplanes flying over the London suburbs and the unremitting hum of traffic. Well, it was silent apart from George Clooney crooning to his girls who were clucking for their breakfast, and Brad Pitt, a handsome cockerel, trying to engage his younger brothers Ronnie and Reggie Kray in a crow-off, which got all the village cockerels going. It's a sound you need to get used to if you live in the countryside. There have been issues with city slickers wanting a bucolic life without some of the rustic accoutrements, and newspapers have reported conflicts taking place all over France as 'neo-rurals' have tried to bring legal action to suppress crowing cockerels, ringing church bells, tinkling cowbells, croaking frogs and so-called 'unbearable' smells from cattle farms!

The doorbell rang, which woke the dogs who barked loudly, which woke the cats who shot up the garden and made a flock of doves sitting in a tree – who had been patiently waiting for me to fill up the wild bird feeders – burst into the sky. It was Petit Frère, who had come to tell us that he'd paid an early visit to the boulangerie to get some croissants, pains aux raisins and pains au chocolat for a committee breakfast meeting at the *salle des fêtes*.

We followed him down the hill. The air was scented by the spring roses that grow outside all the houses, up walls, over fences and around doorways. Thierry the farmer went by in his tractor, stopping briefly to say '*bonjour*' and assure us that he would be taking a couple of hours off to join us at the town hall later for Claudette's party. She's the biggest landowner in the area and several farmers rent land from her, so they'd all been invited.

In the large room at the back of the town hall, Jean-Claude had been leaning back in a chair with his cap pulled down and his eyes closed until the aroma of the just-baked croissants reached him, when he sat forward with a smile. Bernadette had a pot of coffee on the go in the little kitchen and we drank thick espressos and feasted on the sweet pastries while Bernadette ran through the jobs one more time: she was leaving nothing to chance.

Everything went like clockwork. I picked up the cheeses, including local Maroilles, which meant driving with all the car windows open because it's so smelly. But you simply cannot have a party here without stinky cheese.

Cheese is a symbol of France and a serious topic: it's not just something you buy in a packet, pop in the fridge and unwrap from its plastic layering when you want to eat it. Cheese is one of the things that defines Frenchness. The fact that Mark is allergic to cheese garners him a lot of pity, but also means he will never be truly accepted. And I will only ever make it halfway as I am allergic to the mould in blue cheese – it makes my tongue swell to an unattractively large size, as I discovered while tasting a tangy Roquefort at a food fair in Calais. A sliver of this 'King of the Blues' turned me into a gibbering idiot.

The French get through a whopping 58 pounds of cheese per person, per year – incredibly, that's more than three times the amount of chocolate they consume. Apparently, 47 per cent of French people eat cheese on a daily basis. Children even discuss the cheese they had for lunch; to an outsider, it is very odd to hear a pair of four-year-olds announce that they had eaten a really good Camembert at school that day – I'm not even kidding, I overheard them chatting at the village bus stop. French school lunches are the beginning of a journey to a lifelong appreciation of food. From the age of three, either a three- or four-course meal is served, and it's definitely not pizza and chips. There's an emphasis on local, seasonal and organic, and even vegetarian cuisine is becoming more commonplace. French kids enjoy school lunches consisting of dishes such as duck parmentier with organic mashed potatoes and butternut squash or grilled guinea fowl with Provençal herbs and organic cauliflower and broccoli. Tomato ketchup is banned – except if fries are served. And always, there is a cheese course, but we're not talking cheese straws here: bug-ridden Mimolette (banned in the US due to the cheese mites that are introduced to the rind to add extra flavour) and pungent Munster are just as likely as Brie or a soupçon of blue cheese.

Bread Man arrived at the *salle des fêtes* at exactly the right time, and as he carried a basket full of baguettes, the perfect partner for cheese, the aroma of freshly baked bread followed him into the room. The food that had been lovingly prepared throughout the village for days before was being stored in the cool kitchen. Tables and chairs were set up in the large courtyard of the town hall, and the DJ, with a deck worthy of Ibiza's finest clubs, was ensconced in a corner next to a tub of flowers. The wines and glasses were delivered by a jovial man from a local *cave*, a store specializing in wine and spirits, who said that the best wines are the ones we drink with our friends, and he was quite certain that we would be more than satisfied with the reds and whites he had carefully chosen.

Five local teenagers arrived to be drilled in their duties by Bernadette, which were to lay the food out on a long table at 11.30 and then cover it with cloths until everyone was ready to eat. They were to bring wine to the tables as needed and keep it all tidy. A smiling Bernadette said that everything had gone even better than she'd hoped, and even Jean-Claude got a 'good job' from her, though he had done little but sit and read out the chores that needed doing, ticking them off his long list one by one.

'Right, let's all go home to get ready, and we will meet back here at eleven-thirty. Then I will go and get *Maman* and bring her here for midday.' Bernadette turned to look at Jean-Claude, who is always late for everything.

'Of course, my little *choupinette*, my cute little cabbage,' he grinned. The sun and the chance to celebrate with Claudette was making us all happy.

By the time we had returned to the *salle des fêtes*, the courtyard was already teeming with guests exchanging kisses and chatting animatedly. Just before noon, the DJ asked everyone to be quiet: the guest of honour was arriving. When Bernadette led Claudette into the courtyard, there was cheering and clapping, and Jean-Claude, for once not dressed in his usual hunting-green trousers and jumper, but instead sporting wide-bottomed jeans and a Johnny Hallyday T-shirt, started everyone singing a rousing rendition of '*Bon Anniversaire*'.

Claudette was pink-faced as she looked around at everyone standing there smiling at her.

It was one of those afternoons when you feel that all is good with the world. Claudette's nearest and dearest were there. Ruddy-faced farmers and their rosy-cheeked wives, old ladies in cardigans and wizened old men telling tales of yesteryear, and two nuns dressed in grey habits who had arrived on bicycles, all sat on rickety chairs and stools, borrowed from across the village for the occasion. People were perched at different heights, with Jean-Claude towering atop the tallest of the bar stools, swaying precariously and clutching his glass of pastis, determined not to spill a drop.

Wooden boards covered with colourful cloths served as tables and jam jars were filled with wild flowers of all kinds – bright blue cornflowers, buttercups, daisies and purple bluebells, alongside pots of lily of the valley. Colourful balloons were tied to trees, the backs of chairs and the end of the long table heaving with dishes of food. Occasionally a balloon popped, making everyone jump.

Jean-Claude had made dozens of bug traps fashioned from plastic water bottles containing sugar water to make sure unwelcome visitors didn't spoil the day, but, being short, he'd hung them only as high as his arms could reach – which was the lowest branches of the trees that encircled the courtyard. So, anyone taller than him – which was most people – kept smacking their heads on them. Jean-François, the village handyman, shouted '*olé*' as his forehead hit one of the pesky traps, and thereafter if anyone else made the same mistake, cries of '*olé*' rang out from the partygoers.

We tucked into the pies and pastries. We mopped up delectable sauces that would make a Michelin-starred chef proud, cleaning our plates with chunks of bread. And we savoured smelly, sweaty, succulent cheeses that were warmed to perfection by the sun.

When the DJ put on ABBA's 'Dancing Queen', the nuns, who looked to be in their seventies, leaped to their feet, dashed to the dance floor and began to enthusiastically spin around, do the locomotion and beat their imaginary tambourines. Never did the words dancing, jiving and having the time of your life seem more appropriate. The nimble nuns never left the dance floor. They boogied to every song the DJ played and I'm pretty sure he was testing them when he put on The Prodigy's feisty 'Firestarter' – but, undeterred, they carried on. Everyone left their seats to dance to 'Le Madison', a crowd-pleasing, line-dancing anthem beloved in France since the late 1950s. Claudette held hands with the dancing nuns and carefully picked out the steps, earning a loud cheer as she returned to her seat. As usual, a medley of songs by the late, great Johnny Hallyday – the French Elvis – caused a stampede to the dance floor, while older guests sat around tapping their feet and nodding their heads.

As evening fell, I made my way to the town hall's little kitchen to make the end-of-party cocktail – La Claudette. The year before, I'd been asked to be a judge at a Calvados cocktail contest in Caen (and try saying that after you've tasted twenty of them, as I did that day) as well as attending a tasting workshop beginning at 8.30 that same morning. Calvados is a sort of apple brandy, a speciality of the Calvados department in Normandy. In the old days, it was customary to have a little drop with your morning coffee, but now it's more popular as an after-dinner drink. For the contest, dozens of bartenders from around the world prepared cocktails in a darkened venue, using vegetables, fruit, mixers and Calvados. They swung and tossed bottles like jugglers in a circus, TV cameras zoomed in to catch the drama as they blended, jiggled and rattled their concoctions. Teams of judges huddled together and sipped, discussed, debated and awarded points until a winner was chosen. I came away a fan of Calvados cocktails, so Bernadette had asked me to make something for Claudette.

Sixty-eight glasses were set out, and into each went a finger of Calvados, a dollop of strawberry syrup, some orange juice and soda water, garnished with fresh strawberries from the Montéchor strawberry farm close by.

The teenage servers delivered the cocktails to the tables, the DJ played '*Bon Anniversaire*' and our voices echoed around the valley as we lifted our glasses to toast Claudette. As Bernadette and Jean-Claude carefully wheeled a trolley into the courtyard, upon which was sat a huge croquembouche cake – a towering pyramid of cream-filled choux pastry puffs held together with spun sugar the colour of a late summer sunset, with sparklers all around it spitting silver and gold – a collective '*Oh là là*' went up from the crowd.

'Speech, speech!' cried Petit Frère – Claudette is well known for her wise words, even in a village full of wise old people. The DJ passed her a microphone and she looked around at us all with a smile on her face and then spoke in a soft voice.

'I've lived nine decades, all of them here in this village, all of them in the house where I was born, where I lived with my beloved parents when I married, brought my daughter into the world and said goodbye for now to my darling husband. I have lived through war and through occupation. I've witnessed huge change in this little village over the years: television, telephones, electricity in all our houses. I've not travelled far; I've never been to Paris. But everything I hold dear is here in this village and that has never changed. I have reached this grand age, and if you will permit an old lady to share what she has learned, it is this: don't waste time on things that don't matter, try not to spend too much time on things you don't enjoy and remember that today is the most important day of your life, for yesterday is over and tomorrow is yet to come. The most important thing in life is love. It is a wonderful thing to be loved – and better still to love. You are all so dear to me, my family, my friends.'

'Bravo!' called Jean-Claude as he dabbed his eyes with his jacket sleeve, and some of the tough old farmers sniffed softly.

By seven o'clock, Claudette was ready to leave – it was her bedtime, and she swears that an early night and a small glass of cider with breakfast is what gives her her youthful energy. She never changes her routine.

Not for the first time, I thanked the lucky stars that had steered us to this tiny village in the middle of nowhere, northern France. We had no idea then what lay in store for us: a chance meeting with an estate agent while on a day trip to buy wine led us to acquire a neglected farmhouse, starting a chain of events that were to change our lives.

We had bought a ruin, but we had found a home.

CHAPTER 2

La vie en rose

WHEN MARK'S GRANDDAD retired from being a fireman in London, he took a part-time job that suited his passion for gardening. He worked for wealthy clients, including bankers, actors and even a Saudi prince, who all had grand homes with large gardens in London. After a morning spent weeding, pruning and planting in a client's garden, he would sit with his corned beef and pickle sandwiches and a flask of tea and soak up the beauty. He admired the colourful, scented flower beds and the vegetable gardens whose bounty only he would enjoy, the owners having neither the time nor the inclination to pick and prepare the fruits of the gardener's labour. He listened to birdsong and loved the seasons, the smell of rain and the warmth of the sun. He would sigh with satisfaction over the immaculate, perfectly edged and trimmed pea-green lawns on which sat cooing pigeons waiting for him to throw a crumb or two.

'You know,' he would say to Mark, 'these people work very long hours and earn lots of money. They can afford to buy whatever they want, and they think that they have got everything that's worth having. And yet I'm the one sitting there enjoying what they've paid for.'

He never went to France but he would have fit right in – he had the right philosophy. In France, living your best life is all about living in the moment and making it as good as it can be. It is known by several names: *joie de vivre* (the joy of life), *la belle vie* (the good life), *art de vivre* (the art of living). It is the art of appreciating beautiful things. It's taking the time to admire a place, the efforts that someone has gone to in order to create a delicious dish or a good wine. The good life is something that encompasses small pleasures and big celebrations.

It's time spent with family or going to a cultural event. It's sitting at a table on the pavement outside a café with nothing to do except sip black coffee from a pure white cup and watch the world go about its business. It's taking time to appreciate a beautifully laid table, a neatly folded linen napkin or three perfect wedges of cheese on a plate. It's nibbling the end of a baguette on the way home from the boulangerie or sharing a bottle of wine with friends. The good life is about embracing life to its fullest or, as the French say, *croquer la vie à pleines dents* (literally: 'bite into life with all your teeth').

We never forgot what we called the 'Granddad Trap', the ability to appreciate what you have and to make the most of it, though the old man had been gone more than thirty years by the time we had moved to

France. We went for the good life, to spend more time together, to explore our adopted country, to grow our own vegetables and live in a way that wasn't all about work and money. But we are not millionaires: we need to earn money to pay the bills, to eat, to take care of our animals. And the longer we are here, the more we realize that it's not just a question of wanting to live the good life – you also have to work at it and make time for it.

When I began blogging in 2012, I had absolutely no idea what I was doing. But to my great surprise, the website I began as a way of keeping in touch with family started to attract more and more readers. I was invited to visit different places in France and write about my travels for my website, The Good Life France, as well as for newspapers, magazines and books. Mark, who is not as keen on travel as me, was happy to stay at home to look after our ever-expanding animal family.

It was Mark who built the website in the first place, and the whole process of creating websites, understanding how they work and fathoming the psychology of sales through the internet fascinated him. He started to develop websites for other people and became an expert digital marketer. We had terrible internet service in our village, which made it almost impossible for Mark to work from home. He went to the UK each month to meet clients, and eventually spent more and more time working there.

We weren't getting rich by any means, but with Mark away so much, we started to find that we didn't have enough time to work in the garden growing vegetables or finish renovating the house. That sustainable way of life, the good life we'd envisaged, was starting to slip away. Listening to Claudette's speech about not leaving things until it's too late reminded us that we had to make a conscious effort to live the life we wanted. I've lost count of the number of people I've met who moved to France to experience a more laid-back lifestyle and to have more time for each other and family, only to moan that they have just as little time as they did before. Managing a *gîte*, running a business and working are just as time-consuming in France as anywhere else – if not more so, taking into account the famous French administration. So the day the mayor announced that we would be getting high-speed internet after a ten-year battle to propel our village into the twenty-first century was life-changing. It meant we could both work from home. The Good Life was back on track.

When we first bought our house in France, it was intended to be our holiday home. Purchased on a whim, it required Mark to sell his beloved Jaguar car and both of us to give up anything that cost money and wasn't a necessity for many years.

'It's a bit neglected. Needs modernizing and a new roof,' the estate agent had told us. 'It doesn't have mains drains. Some rooms have earth floors. It could do with new windows ... and doors. It needs a bit of work, to tell the truth.'

It was a hovel. But it was a hovel that pulled at my heart strings the moment I looked out over the huge garden with fields at the bottom, an ancient church spire reaching up to the sky in the distance, bells ringing. Ducks quacked in a garden nearby, wild birds flew overhead. A tiny stream gently meandered through the village and all around were hills; this was, after all, the Seven Valleys. It was the perfect image of my dream of bucolic countryside. I focused on the good, not the bad. But there was no getting away from the fact that the property needed a huge amount of work.

We started by laying concrete floors inside the house as well as outside for the cars, which were apt to sink into the mud when left overnight. We bought a tractor: it was small, cheap and a lovely shiny bright blue. With just the two of us doing all the renovations, we hoped it would help to make the work less onerous. We also purchased a modestly sized trailer for its transportation to France – the cheapest we could find – but when the tractor was delivered in a trailer that was four times larger than the one we had just bought, we knew we had a major problem. Although the tractor was small, it was still much bigger than the large ride-on lawnmower we'd envisaged. And with a loader bucket on the front and a digger mechanism on the back, it was too long for our little trailer. We persuaded the delivery men to loan us theirs for twenty-four hours, so that we could take the tractor to France and return their trailer the next day, along with several bottles of wine.

We headed off to the Eurotunnel train terminal in Kent, stopping briefly to pick up my dad who lived near to us and who accompanied us on trips to France whenever he could. He whistled when he saw the tractor: 'It's bigger than the car – how the hell are we going to drag that all the way to France?' He had a point. It was worrying me as well.

'It'll be fine,' said Mark, assuring us both that our 4x4 would be able to cope.

'You've got yourself a bit of ground out there, you can plant potatoes and dig 'em up with that tractor. Go and work for the local council digging ditches,' suggested Dad, on a roll now. 'You'll never get it through the gates to the garden. And as for storing it in the garage, you can forget that. It's bloody huge.'

He kept this up for an hour and a half all the way down the motorway to Folkestone. Things didn't improve when we arrived. Although the authorities let you take through pretty much whatever you liked in terms of volume back then, a policeman at the check-in point wanted to see the registration details for the tractor.

'We don't have any. We only bought it three hours ago,' Mark explained.

'You can't drive it on the road if you don't have registration details.'

'We don't want to drive it on the road. We want to transport it on a trailer to France.'

'How do we know you didn't steal it if you don't have a logbook?'

'Look at it, bloody great thing. We wouldn't be driving around with it in plain sight if we'd stolen it,' said Dad reasonably.

'I need proof it's yours,' replied the policeman.

We offered to phone the tractor company, but it was after hours and a cleaner answered the phone. She gave us the managing director's home phone number, but he couldn't help. 'I sell a lot of tractors. I can't remember the names of the buyers and I don't take the invoices home,' he said. Dad kept up his commentary on how ridiculously large the tractor was and how much work the house needed, and on the balance of probabilities – that we had the tractor company's details and were with an old man who couldn't keep quiet – they finally let us go.

To reach our little village, we have to drive up and down the hellishly steep hills that crowd the land between Boulogne-sur-Mer and Desvres. A mountain goat might baulk at the inclines, but not Mark. The weight of the tractor pushed the car down the hills and then dragged it almost to a standstill on the upward sections. Even Dad was quiet for this bit of the journey, eyes closed, one hand gripping the door.

We finally arrived in pitch-darkness. Mark drove the

tractor off the trailer and Dad directed him as he tried to reverse into the garage but instead went straight into the wall, creating a huge crack. It's still there; we like the reminder.

The tractor became a bit of a novelty in the village – no one had ever seen one that small. Jean-Claude later roped us in to help dig out the village boules pitch. The tractor was a star: it dug, it pulled the oak beams that someone had donated to line the pitch with, and the loader bucket made a great picnic table when we took a break. Jean-Claude demanded that the mayor should give us several litres of diesel as a thank-you for our labour. We didn't want it – and couldn't use it – but Jean-Claude made him cough up: a matter of principle, he said, and besides, if we didn't need it he would happily take it off our hands.

But when we left the tractor alone for a while, it seemed to have abandonment issues. It wouldn't start, the hose broke and it leaked thick oil, which 'Enry Cooper the cat managed to wipe over the top of his mouth as if trying to paint on a moustache – it made him look like a furry Clark Gable. The steering column leaked and we replaced the battery three times. Once the major digging work was over, we sold it to a local builder – he says it's been as good as gold ever since.

The builder came back to see us one day to ask if we had any spare pram wheels. 'Perhaps some bike wheels?' he asked hopefully. We didn't, but we told him that we knew someone who might, thinking of our English friends Gary and Annette, who are very good at keeping things that might come in handy thirty years down the line.

You might think that few newsworthy events take place in the little villages and hamlets of northern France, and you'd be mostly right, but you'd also be wrong. It's true that if you pick up a local newspaper, the pages will normally contain a photo of some schoolchildren playing football, reports on regional politics or a story about a new mayor being elected in a village nearby, and there's always something about the weather. On rare occasions there is more gripping news, such as the Tour de France passing through the Seven Valleys or the sighting of a swarm of bees.

And yes, it is rather sleepy. Locals look up if a car goes by, and they usually know the driver and receive a cheery wave or a nod. But behind that serene façade, there can be a whole lot of drama going on.

'I don't suppose you've got any old sheets of wood you don't want? I want to pimp my soapbox,' said the builder. Now that's not something you hear often. 'I'm making a soapbox car,' he explained, 'for an important race. But I've got no wheels ...' He pulled a piece of paper out of his pocket and showed us a drawing of what was essentially a wood palette with two wheels on each side and a stick with a steering wheel in the front.

Mark took him up to the workshop to look for

wood and they were gone for an hour. Apparently, they discussed aerodynamics, speed, brakes, slipstreams, streamlining and other aspects of racing, and as soon as the builder found out that Mark used to be a car mechanic, he roped him in to help with the creation of his racing car.

During the construction of the car – which would ultimately resemble a small shed on wheels that featured hooks on the outside for tools to hang from, an extra detail to reflect the builder's vocation – Mark would disappear with him for hours on end. The pair of them stripped down a lawnmower that someone had thrown out, which was good for the steering gear, while Gary and Annette did indeed provide the wheels. The would-be car makers preened, painted and prepared, and when their creation was deemed roadworthy, they tested it on a hill in the small town of Hucqueliers, reasoning that if it was good enough for the Tour de France a few years previously, it was good enough for Shed Car.

Several weeks later, we headed to a nearby village to watch the builder race his shed down a steep, hay-bale-lined hill with several twists and turns. Along the route people hung out of windows and stood along the side of the road. A band played rousing music and from a food tent came enticing barbecue smells. Many of our neighbours were there to cheer the crazy pilots on – it's all about community, sharing experiences and *joie de vivre*.

Two tractors dragged the cars over to the starting position at the top of the hill. It was to be a race against the clock, with vehicles setting off every few seconds in an attempt to avoid too much of a pile-up. The band began to play the stirring theme music from the *Rocky* film and then they were off – at a rather sedate pace to start with, but gaining speed as they hit the steep bends.

Some karts had a single driver, while others had a driver and passenger. There was good-natured rivalry between the teams of the *gendarmes* (police) and the *pompiers* (firefighters), of whom the latter were always the favourites, with everyone cheering as the miniature fire engine hurtled down the hill, then ooh'ing and ahh'ing as the petite patrol car complete with flashing lights attempted to catch up.

A tiny Formula One kart overtook the builder's shed with ease, caught up with the *pompiers* and *gendarmes* and sped to the finish line. The diminutive driver was dressed in a white racing suit with a white helmet and black visor. The signage on the vehicle referenced a local garage, which was known to lose every year much to the chagrin of the owner. Had he brought in The Stig from *Top Gear*, we wondered, a ringer, a racing driver? The garage's car raced down the hill in all three heats and won every time.

'He's going faster than you in a Ferrari,' Mark said to me, laughing. And he was right. The week before I'd been to Mulhouse in Alsace where I visited the famous car museum. I've never been anywhere quite like it. I'm no petrolhead but it's extraordinary, with a collection of 450 or so mostly European cars from 1878 onwards. Steam-engine cars, classic cars, racing cars and celebrity cars, including Charlie Chaplin's gleaming 1924 Rolls-Royce Silver Ghost and Ettore Bugatti's own Bugatti Type 41 Coupé Napoleon (one of only six in the world and so rare it can't be valued). There's also a private racing track where you can test-drive a selection of iconic cars – I chose a Ferrari. I confessed to Mark that I was too scared to go over 50 kilometres an hour round the track, despite the encouragement of the bemused track manager who told me afterwards that he'd never seen anything quite like it. And now here was a man in a home-made wooden box with no engine beating my time by coasting down a narrow hill in the middle of nowhere.

A frenzied commentator bellowed out a muffled critique of the race, screaming with laughter whenever a car bashed into a hay bale or tipped over (no one was hurt). At one point he dropped the microphone with a loud thud, and after that screeching feedback punctuated his commentary, causing everyone to cover their ears and groan.

We never did find out who the speedy driver was; they apparently had to leave before the prize-giving, and to this day their identity remains a mystery. But the garage was the eventual winner and the proud owner duly accepted the prize. The shed was beaten by a snail, a peanut and a steam train. 'No worries,' said the builder. 'It's way better than I've ever done before. There's always next year … I think we should build a car in the shape of a drill – it will be more streamlined.'

In the food tent, a rotund, red-faced chef with a twirly moustache was presiding over a hog roast. His white cook's jacket was plastered in grease from the roast, but the toque on his head was spotless. Chefs are proud of their toques. The taller the white hat, the more important the reputation of the chef. In days gone by, the hat would feature folds: the more folds, the more ways a cook knew how to prepare an egg – it could be up to a hundred folds! The great French chef Auguste Escoffier once said: 'The spotless white straight toque and uniform are synonymous with cleanliness and moral rectitude and aim to inspire confidence among restaurant clients.' I'm not sure what he would have made of our sweaty chef, who was wielding a long knife like the musketeer d'Artagnan as he carved slices from the hog and thwacked them on plates, to which his two assistants added a wodge of steaming hot *frites* and a brioche bun. On the table was an array of exotic-sounding sauces, including Samurai (which, despite its name, is from Belgium and traditionally served with *frites*), and for the really adventurous there was Biggy Burger Sauce, which is a sort of garlicky pickle (also from Belgium), as well as a curry mayonnaise.

In between bouts of carving, the chef helped himself to a slice or two, rolling his eyes in delight as he munched with piggish abandon. Behind him, in a van, the fattest dog you've ever seen in your life hung out of the window, drool dangling from his open mouth as he watched his master serve the happy punters; he knew he would get the leftovers later, lucky dog. It was the best hog roast we've ever tasted.

Year round there is a huge number of diverse events and celebrations that bring communities together. There is fierce competition to be crowned the grower of the biggest pumpkin in the valleys, to produce the best tart, to make the most artistic straw sculpture, to cultivate the juiciest strawberry, the tallest sunflower or the longest cucumber. Strangely, the longest baguette ever baked was in Italy, not France, in 2015. At a whopping 122 metres (400 feet) long, it took sixty French and Italian bakers almost seven hours to make.

'*Waouh*,' said Bread Man, which is French for 'wow', when I told him about it. He wrinkled his brow and worked out that the average family on his round eats a baguette every day of the week. And that at an average of 65 centimetres long, that works out to almost 240 metres of bread per family per year. Bread Man nodded slowly at me, one eye closed. He doesn't win accolades or awards, but he is definitely a champion in this part of France.

But it's the rose-growing contest that really gets temperatures rising in this neck of the woods. Every year at a local fair, a competition is held for the prettiest rose. There are usually about twenty-five people who take part and they come from villages for miles around to show off their blooms.

Rosa gallica, which means 'rose of Gaul' or Gallic rose, was one of the first rose species cultivated in central Europe and is the ancestor of all modern roses. Also known as the 'rose of Provins', it was said to have been brought to France in 1240 by Thibaut IV, Count of Champagne, upon his return from the Barons' Crusade wearing a rose in his helmet, and the people of France have had a love affair with roses ever since.

In the 1700s, the French took to the breeding of roses with gusto and by 1800 they had produced more than 5,000 varieties. Joséphine, wife of Napoléon Bonaparte, was crazy for them, so Napoléon instructed his captains to seek out roses on their travels around the world. Back in France, they were cross-bred and hybridized, leading to today's 30,000 varieties and counting. Joséphine's garden was filled with roses and she started a trend that continues to this day. The rose variety 'Empress Joséphine' is named after her – a bright-pink, fruity-fragranced beauty. Rose gardens are so popular in France that there are even entire villages filled with roses.

The passion for these plants is palpable among local competitors. Rumours regarding the lengths they will go to in their efforts to cultivate them abound. The wife of one grower is aware that her beloved certainly has more ardour for a full-bodied, carmine-coloured beauty of a rose named after Baron Girod de l'Ain, a French politician who has been dead since 1847, than for her. 'He remembers when he bought that rose, but he can't recall our children's birthdays,' she complained. A husband-and-wife rose-growing team talk of nothing else. They spend their days pruning, spraying, fertilizing, repotting, disbudding, picking bugs off with tweezers, examining and even talking to their roses. And when the blooming season is over, they plant more roses and talk about that. There is even gossip that the wife of a rose-obsessed competitor ended her marriage on the grounds that her husband exhibited an 'unhealthy passion' for Cardinal de Richelieu (a deep purple-red rose).

'You should take part in the contest,' said Mark, eyeing my sprawling mass of pink, white and red roses. 'They look rather good.'

Yet again I'd allowed them to get out of control and reach such heights that they were poking through the guttering, growing over windows and shutters and sprawling across the pathway. I'd planted them just a few years previously and they were thriving in the northern climate.

'I can't enter this year,' I said. 'I've just received an invitation to help judge the next contest.'

It's one of the strange side effects of writing books: people seem to think you're an expert in things you very often know little about. I've been a judge at several cake and tart competitions – in which I actually am an expert, in that I have eaten many over the years. But roses? I knew nothing, but I asked myself, 'How hard can it be to judge the beauty of a flower?'

The day of the fair came round. Organized within the shady avenues of a local château and spreading out into the gardens and a meadow, stalls were set up selling second-hand goods, plants of all sorts, locally grown salad, fruit and vegetables, cheese, dairy and charcuterie. In one area, old farm equipment was laid out and admirers thronged to appreciate the fine lines of a pitchfork, the strong handle of a potato planter and the sharp edge of a scythe. A barn became a rustic bistro, with tables and chairs spilling out into a courtyard. The whirring of a chainsaw sculptor came from one end of the castle grounds, and from the other the roar of old tractors revving up to the delight of the crowds.

In one corner, a man carved fruit into extraordinary shapes and patterns, creating faces in bananas and parrots in pineapples, teddy bears made from oranges and intricately carved melons that looked like lacy flowers. A large crowd gathered as he transformed an apple into a swan with red-tipped wings, and there was a rush to buy sets of carving knives from him when he had finished. I like to imagine that in the kitchens of northern France, there are legions of old ladies whittling furiously away, addicted to transforming cucumbers into camels and pumpkins into pirate ships ...

In the centre of the grand château's courtyard was the tent in which the roses were to be displayed – and judged. My fellow appraisers were the château owners (a rose-enthusiast couple with an enviable collection – the perfect choice to make such an important decision) and a local nursery owner who specialized in roses.

Contestants arrived to place their cut blooms in plain glass vases on a long table. They were assigned a card with a number. All entries were anonymous; in the cut-throat cut-rose world, there are highly stringent rules to be followed.

When the time came for judging, the four of us met in the tent, and the château owners led us from rose to rose. Milord sported red trousers, a white shirt, a red cravat and a patched-up blue blazer, while Milady was elegant in a flowing tunic, cropped trousers and ballet flats. The nursery judge had also clearly got the dress code memo as he was wearing smart trousers and a shirt. I stuck out like a sore thumb, clad in rubber boots, jeans and a T-shirt.

They sniffed, looked intently, discussed the merits of the petals, the stems, the width, the depth, the hues of the bloom, and more. They made copious notes and chewed the ends of their pens. We had twenty-three roses to judge. It took more than an hour. I could have done it in five minutes. I marked my paper based on the smell and the colour. At the end we compared notes and, to my amazement, we had all come to the same conclusion. I'm not sure that I'll be asked back, though – they were disappointed by my lack of rose knowledge and my alacrity in scoring the blooms.

There wasn't enough room in the tent to make the presentations, so we carried the roses outside to be placed on a table in the courtyard as a crowd gathered. There was no idle chit-chat between competitors; this was serious business. Especially for two of the rose growers – Milord had told me that they lived in the same village and had been at loggerheads for years over the rose-growing contest. Both had won several times and the rivalry between them was fierce. They had forbidden their wives to speak to each other – neither, of course, took any notice of their husbands. They would, if they could, said Milord, even forbid their children to play together – but this is not *West Side Story*, it's a little village in northern France and the children simply ignored the thorny issue that remained ongoing between their fanatical fathers.

As the moment came to deliver the verdict, the adversaries stood on opposite sides of the courtyard. Milord read out the name of the fourth-place winner, a lady with a large straw hat whose luscious pink Madame Pompadour was a real crowd-pleaser. Third place went to an elderly couple for their pink-and-white-striped Henri Matisse.

The feuding rose growers were standing stock-still, ready to either grin in victory or slink away in disgust.

'For the first time in the history of the contest,' said Milord, 'we have a situation. The judges could not agree on who deserved to win and so our esteemed guest judge, Janine Marsh, a local writer, was asked to pick the final winner. And after much deliberation, she is unable to choose between the Mona Lisa and the Empress Joséphine – it is a tie.' There was polite applause, but neither victor was happy.

'What does she know about roses?' remarked one to the other as they came forward to collect their prizes. At last, they were in agreement about something. Thus ended the war of the roses.

CHAPTER 3

Neighbours, everybody needs good neighbours

ONE MIDSUMMER'S DAY, an administrative note from the town hall was pushed into our postbox, which is set into an old stone bread oven in what is now the woodshed in the front garden. Printed in bold type on a piece of paper the shade of putrid pink were the words: '*Le Stade* will be opened this weekend, come in numbers ...'

Almost every invitation we receive to a public event will exalt us to 'come in numbers', by which they mean: 'We'd really love it if lots of you show some support.' Sometimes, to make a point, it will say '*venez en grand nombre*' ('come in big numbers'), which I always take to mean that we'd better be there or else it will be noted on a file at the town hall that we are not good citizens.

The pink leaflet informed us that a group of municipal councillors would join the mayor for a ribbon-cutting ceremony to officially open the *stade*, after which there would be a demonstration of football skills by the local kids, followed by a *vin d'honneur* – a glass of wine in honour of the event – at the town hall next door.

It also laid out exactly how much money had been paid for the *stade*, and where the money had come from in state and local grants, and under what law the subsidies had been applied for. It's a peculiarly French thing to provide so much detail; it makes me wonder if my neighbours are busy checking such things, discussing the mind-boggling minutiae of municipal budgeting over dinner. Are they enjoying a glass of pastis while poring over the cost of the repaired storm drains in the road that leads from the hill to the village? Or, for fun, checking the price paid for the petunia plants in the flowerpots on the town hall windowsills?

I could, if you were interested, tell you how much, to the exact cent, it cost to replace the slate roof of the ancient village church after it was destroyed by the now legendary hailstorm. Or the rate of mending a pothole in the road outside the home of Monsieur and Madame Pepperpot, an elderly and petite couple who live just off the rue de la Chapelle, a street named in honour of a tiny chapel that's just big enough to allow six worshippers to kneel before a stone altar. Made from chalk blocks, the chapel has been there for several centuries, topped by a white stone statue of a rather smiley-faced St Adrien dressed as a Roman soldier – which he was before converting to Christianity and becoming a saint (one of a group of saints, in fact, who it was believed protected people against the plague).

Often accompanying these rainbow-coloured missives from the mayor are letters from the providers of various services, detailing the precise particulars of the actions they will be undertaking and an explanation of the costs. It all points to a sort of communal responsibility that's particularly strong in rural areas.

Life in the countryside is all about sharing: it requires one to be neighbourly. It's not like living in a city or town. Back in London, I hardly ever spoke to my neighbours. In crowded towns, space is at a premium and fiercely protected. The lady who lived next door to my house used to catch the same train as me into central London, where we both worked, and yet we only ever nodded to each other. We carried on this way for several years. Living in the middle of nowhere, in a village in rural France with a population of fewer than 150 people, is a very different experience. Everyone talks to everyone (generally about each other) and it is very much a community. If you want to fit in, you'd better be prepared to turn up to almost every occasion to which you receive an invite.

Jean-Claude is always dragging us into something or other. Catching rats, building a boules pitch, digging potatoes, repairing doors, cutting wood, helping to push his temperamental tractor down the hill to get it started when it won't fire up. Ever since we arrived in the village, he's made sure that we are included in all that goes on. He may have occasionally laughed at our efforts to become self-sufficient, but he and our other neighbours have been nothing less than patient when we ask daft questions, and they are good-natured and generous both with their advice and the bounty from their gardens.

Sometimes Jean-Claude will have a bit of fun at our expense, telling us villagers' nicknames that are often cheeky and, in one memorable case, downright offensive. The latter instance led to an unfortunate and long-term contretemps between me and a neighbour, back when I didn't know Jean-Claude well enough to check things out before going full steam ahead into believing and repeating everything he told me. Eventually the neighbour, whose name was Paul, forgave me for referring to him as 'Popaul' – a vulgar term for 'penis' – which Jean-Claude had told me all of his friends called him. Villagers are very good at holding a grudge. A perceived slight can result in neighbours not talking for years. Even though my village is sparsely populated, there are seven hunting clubs as a result of someone not getting on with someone else at various times in the past.

Madame R. was an old lady who used to live opposite the local church, though she moved a while back to be with her daughter in the Loire Valley. Jean-Claude warned us that she was known to hold many grudges and was a difficult woman who liked nothing better than to stir up trouble. One morning as we walked the dogs, she was in her front garden pruning the tidy flower beds. We said '*bonjour*' and went to continue on our way.

'Young man, young man,' she called, which made us smile. Only in a village of elderlies would a chap over fifty be called 'young man'. 'Young man, could you help me please?'

Of course, we turned back. Madame R. was petite and I got the impression that a blast of wind blowing through the Seven Valleys might easily lift her off her feet. She had wispy white hair, rosy cheeks and twinkling blue eyes behind her dark-framed glasses. Madame R. told us that she had an outdoor bench she wanted moving but there was no one to help her. After we'd shifted it from one end of the garden to the other, she invited us in for coffee. Mark declined as he had to take the dogs home, since Ella Fitzgerald was already encouraging Churchill and Bruno to run circles round us, but I stayed behind. Surely, I thought, Jean-Claude must be pulling my leg: she looked like your quintessential darling-sweet grandmother.

Madame R. didn't have a kitchen – her cooker and sink were in the corner of a dimly lit sitting room in which the shutters were closed to keep the sun out. She made some coffee and poured it into tiny china cups, and as soon as we sat down, she asked me if I knew of her neighbour, a mother with three children. I was about to answer yes, and that I liked her very much, when Madame R. revealed that she detested her neighbour. The woman had once had a barbecue and the smoke had blown into Madame R.'s garden, which prompted her to send a letter to the mayor to complain. She didn't like the mayor, since he had taken no notice of her correspondence. She didn't like children, especially those of her neighbour – they were too noisy. She didn't like teenagers, as there was one in the village who rode a moped and she didn't like mopeds. There seemed to be no one whom she did like, including her late husband, who was apparently deaf and worked long hours (I soon began to understand why). I sat through it all, barely saying a word, and left as soon as I could. Alas, on a walk with the dogs a week later, they ran through the open gate of her garden and chased her cat, which resulted in a new grudge – she never spoke to us again. Whenever she was outdoors as we passed by, she would disappear into the house and shut the door firmly.

I am terrible at holding a grudge. There are times when Mark and I have blazing debates. When you are miles away from a town and friends, and your family live in a whole other country, it's not so easy to walk out and stay somewhere else when you've had enough, which is what we used to do back in London. Back then, if we rowed I would simply head to the office (one of the perks of working for an American bank that serviced wealthy clients around the world meant that it was never closed to staff or customers). Mark, on the other hand, would throw some clothes into the back of his car and drive off, coming back after a few hours when he had calmed down – he has a much hotter temper than me. Faced with no option other than to get on with things in the middle of nowhere, we have largely learned to get over a quarrel more quickly. Life's too short to hold on to the rotten things – I'd far rather have a head full of happiness.

Jean-Claude rarely holds a grudge – mostly, I suspect, since even if he tried it would likely be washed away by wine, pastis and beer. On a mission to keep out from underneath Bernadette's feet, the merest pretext will suffice as a reason for him to visit us. Often he will say that he felt the need to teach us something about French life, or to share some news from near and far (and by 'far' I mean no more than three villages away).

One afternoon he arrived to tell us that he'd taken on a job for the new-people-who-live-in-the-mansion. He calls them 'the New People', but they've owned the house for the best part of two years (though they don't live there full-time). Rumour has it that they fell in love with the old *maison de maître* on the outskirts of the village while on holiday nearby. The property had once belonged to a wealthy shop owner, and the New People had managed to persuade the elderly sisters who had inherited it several years before, and been leaving it to rot, to sell it to them.

It's incredible to me how long families hold onto properties for in France, and I don't mean those like the British royal family or aristocrats. I'm talking about ordinary people. There is a large farmhouse in the next village which is famous in these parts because the family members who inherited it refuse to sit in the same room as each other and they disagree on everything, including whether to sell it and what price to sell it at if they did. Meanwhile, they have paid taxes and maintenance on the empty house for decades. I've peeped through the windows and discovered that the inside is like a museum dedicated to the 1960s. (In the garage is a Citroën DS, which makes Mark sigh with envy; this car was far ahead of its time with its radical suspension system, apparently.) My neighbour Paul inherited his mother's house ages ago and he visits it once a week. In the summer he keeps the garden tidy, in the winter he lights the wood fire and does a little DIY. He's been doing this for the best part of twenty-five years.

Most people think it's just naive expats who buy old properties and spend ridiculous amounts of money doing them up when they could have bought a new house ready to move into. But there are plenty of French people who are just as unable to resist a renovation or the desire to build a folly (which comes from the French word *folie* meaning 'madness'). I've lost count of the number of castle restoration projects I've come across on my travels, like the gorgeous Château du Rivau in the Loire Valley, which took French couple Patricia and Éric Laigneau many years to restore and create magical gardens in its grounds, or Guédelon, a twenty-first-century medieval-style castle being built to thirteenth-century specifications by locals and volunteers in Yonne in Burgundy, which will take decades to complete. My favourite French folly is the Palais Idéal of Postman Cheval, an incredible building in the Drôme department in the south. It was constructed over the course of thirty-three years by a postman called Ferdinand Cheval, who at the age of forty-three tripped on an unusually shaped stone while delivering mail. He took the stone home and came up with the idea to create his 'ideal palace'. For the next thirty-three years, he collected stones on his postal rounds and, with his bare hands and no formal training, erected a magnificent building, a palace of pebbles, which was completed in 1912. It was an obsession – he barely slept, his neighbours thought him crazy – but it was his dream. I often think of him when I'm pulling flintstones, a geological feature of this area, out of the vegetable patch and one day, I may build my own French folly (unless it takes us thirty-three years to finish the house, in which case I will have run out of steam).

Jean-Claude thinks it is madness to spend so much time and money doing up an old property, and sometimes I think he might be right. After fifteen years, we're still not done.

'About this new job I've taken on,' began Jean-Claude. 'The New People have a couple of horses which they sometimes keep here, and they want me to feed and look after them when they can't. I could do with the extra cash, but I have to go into hospital for a small knee operation, so I'll be out of action for a couple of weeks and they might be away at the same time ...' He trailed off and took an enthusiastic sniff and slurp of the wine that I'd poured him. 'I don't suppose you can help me out and look after them while I'm recuperating? It's only for a few days. I'll be back in action in no time,' he said, revising down the original estimate of two weeks to sweeten the deal, perhaps.

I'm not a horse fan. When I was eleven, I went riding and I thought I was pretty good at it. At the end of the outing, I tried to leap off, got my foot stuck in the stirrup, landed on my head and knocked myself out. Not the horse's fault at all, but it did put me off. Many years later, I went to Tunisia on holiday and attended a Bedouin festival. It was quite a significant event in an enormous marquee with hundreds of tourists in attendance. The Bedouin are renowned for having excellent horsemanship skills, and they rode their steeds with great panache and speed round the tent.

And then they called for volunteers. I did not volunteer. The person who was sitting next to me volunteered me.

I was wearing a strapless dress, which was the fashion then. I think we can all guess what happened next. A swarthy, moustachioed, leather-booted Bedouin man came and plucked me from the audience. I was so stressed that I could hardly breathe and my legs were shaking. He led me down to the sawdust-covered floor of the huge arena, while the audience cheered wildly. He then swung me up into the saddle of the largest horse I've ever seen, leaped on behind me and started galloping as though demons were chasing us. The audience cheered even more wildly and laughed as my fragile, strapless dress reacted to the riding motion, and then they got an eyeful of more than we'd all bargained for before our arrival that evening.

I was eventually allowed to return to my seat, scarlet-faced, trembling and seething with hatred for the person who had volunteered me. That was the last time I got close to a horse apart from feeding the local ponies through a fence.

'Sure,' said Mark to Jean-Claude. 'What do you need us to do?'

'I'll let you know nearer the time – it won't be for a while but if I take the job on I just want to know there's backup if I need it. I'll take you round to meet the New People and show you the ropes first.'

He left with a cheery, '*Salut* and see you tomorrow at the *stade* ...'

On the morning of the *stade*'s grand opening, everyone breathed a sigh of relief that the rain which had been falling unrelentingly for the previous three days had at last stopped. A soft mist enveloped the valleys, drifting almost tenderly over the trees and turning the sun white. But by the time we turned up, the skies were azure. Not much bigger than a tennis court, the stadium, with its recycled rubber flooring, encircled by green wire fences and marked up for football, tennis and basketball games, had blue, white and red ribbons tied across the front of the gate.

The dignitaries, comprising local mayors and council leaders, were huddled together in a small group away from the rest of us, looking uncomfortably hot in their suits and mayoral sashes, and conducting an earnest discussion among themselves.

Almost the entire village had turned out and there were visitors who had come from miles away. Like the rest of France, people round here are passionate about football and we didn't dare miss the chance to show solidarity. The year before, when France had reached the finals of the 2018 World Cup, we'd missed watching the game on a TV hired specifically for the occasion at the town hall, and instead we'd headed to Montreuil-sur-Mer, our local large town. There we had met up with some friends who were visiting from the UK for the weekend after they had read an article I'd written in a magazine about how great it is to live here, and on the spur of the moment they decided to visit and see it for themselves.

We had sat on the packed terrace of Le Caveau bistro in the Place du Général de Gaulle, at one of the extra makeshift tables that had been hastily set up using empty wine barrels and boards. The waiting staff, deftly managing great trays brimming with bottles and glasses, dashed in between the crowded tables packed with punters hoping for a positive result from the French team. The main square was chock-a-block with crowds willing the French players on as they watched the match on huge screens. Though we couldn't see the action from our table, we could tell by the cheers and the sighs what was happening. When a mighty roar went up, we knew it was all over and that France had won. Cars were driven in a cacophonous convoy through the town, tooting their horns in ecstatic victory. Jubilant strangers hugged in the street. People broke into song and danced in praise of Les Bleus. A man with blue, white and red streaks painted across his grinning face gave us a French flag. Everyone who passed our table either kissed us or shook our hands.

Our friends were enchanted by the warmth of the locals. The next day, they explored the town and loved rambling round the high stone ramparts that encircle it, providing views over the glorious countryside: a patchwork quilt of fields and forests dotted with tiny villages. They wandered the cobbled streets, noting the many restaurants and bars that make this a classified *destination gastronomique*. The day after they went house-hunting, and found what they were looking for in the nearby village of La Calotterie where they now live with their two young daughters (who spoke not a word of French when they arrived, but within months sounded like locals).

But back in the village, several people asked us why we had missed the match in the town hall – did we not support France? In truth, though we are not quite French and not quite British, we prefer to think of it as a win-win if either team is victorious. 'Of course they support the French,' said Jean-Claude, as he wandered past with a squeaky wheelbarrow full of vegetables that he'd picked from Claudette's garden to take to Bernadette to boil, bottle and barter. 'They're not daft.'

Meanwhile, at the *stade*, there were, as usual, long speeches by the dignitaries before any action could take place. We listened patiently since it would do no good to sigh about it. After sharing more riveting details of costs, in case we hadn't fully appreciated the paper records that had been posted to all of us, the mayor announced that there was to be a village football team and Jean-François, the local handyman, would be the coach. A match was to be played between our side and a visiting team from a village 6 kilometres away in a month's time. Finally, the mayor took a large pair of scissors, the councillors held the ribbon up, and *snip – le stade* was opened to cheers and applause.

'And now we will have a demonstration of football,' said the mayor.

Kids of several ages and sizes ran onto the brand-new pitch as the mayor blew a whistle and passed a football to them. The children ran about kicking the ball to each other and aiming at the goal, which was protected by a small lad with glasses who didn't seem to know that he was supposed to stop the ball from going past him.

Jean-François stood on the sideline watching the motley players, his eyes narrowed. He had swapped his usual uniform of blue boiler suit and hi-vis jacket for a ZZ Top T-shirt and shorts, out of which his spindly white legs protruded like pipe cleaners. He blew a whistle every few seconds: 'Run, pass, turn ...' he yelled. We left him to it as we all trooped into the *salle des fêtes* for the wine.

On the events noticeboard at the side of the town hall, I noticed a glossy and glamorous poster promoting a glittering evening of illuminations and glitzy entertainment in the valleys that night. A photo of a grand château lit up against a dark sky was obscured by the word '*dégustations*' – tastings. That was all that was needed to persuade me we ought to go.

Before driving over to the light show, which was due to start at 10 p.m., we first made our way to the local *auberge* to have dinner and catch up on the week's gossip. The regulars were all in attendance. Old Monsieur Lafont, who is known locally as Monsieur La-Font-of-All-Knowledge because he has an answer for everything, was sat at a table with a stone jug of water and a small glass of pastis. Honestly, it doesn't matter what the topic is, you will never hear him say: 'I don't know.' Best restaurant in Paris? How to get to Corsica by bike? Make tarte Tatin? Understand the government's strategy on taxes? Okay, I made that last one up – I've never asked Monsieur Lafont about this, but I know he would have an answer and it would take hours. Mind you, you rarely hear anyone French admitting their ignorance of a particular subject. They have an aversion to not knowing something.

Opposite him sat Monsieur Dupont, a retired butcher whose garlic sausage has never been bettered, it's said. He and Monsieur Lafont had been friends for more than fifty years, but never ran out of things to talk about. I told them that I was surprised that Bread Man had delivered bread on *Le Quatorze Juillet*, what we English speakers call Bastille Day, earlier in the month. Monsieur Dupont pulled his ear lobes and sucked his false teeth in. Monsieur Lafont took a deep breath then sighed.

'That's the trouble with young people today,' he said. (Young people? Bread Man is at least fifty!) 'When I was young …'

Monsieur Dupont interrupted him with a snort: 'When you were young? You probably took part in the Revolution,' which prompted everyone to call out, '*Vive la France!*'

'When I was young,' started Monsieur Lafont again,

just as Madame the proprietor emerged from the kitchen at the back of the bar.

'Ha, when you were young, dinosaurs roamed these valleys,' she remarked, and everyone laughed.

'When I was young …' Monsieur Lafont tried again and glared at us all, 'you wouldn't get people delivering bread or have shops open until midday on a national holiday like you do now. If you didn't get the shopping done before the day, you went without.'

All the oldies in the bar nodded in agreement, looking rather pleased at the thought.

He took another deep breath, about to get into his stride, but was interrupted by his mobile phone ringing, playing a tinny rendition of '*La Marseillaise*'. It was his wife: '*Oui, chérie. Oui, chérie. Oui*. Right now? *Immédiatement. Oui, chérie.*'

He hauled himself out of his chair. 'When I was young,' he said, with a touch of sadness, 'your wife couldn't ring you on your mobile phone and tell you to pick up the shopping, stop off to make sure her mother was okay, collect a plant from her friend, and do it now … Ah, the good old days!'

We headed into the restaurant at the rear of the *auberge*. Big enough for thirty guests, it's full every week – not because the food is irresistible, but because people want to make sure the place survives. Over the years, bars (particularly those that offer food) have been closing at an alarming rate. Just fifty years ago, every village in the

Seven Valleys had a bar, but now we must drive miles to reach one, and we do so because with local support we can help to keep them open.

It's not a fancy place. The wooden tables, which have seen better days, are covered with white paper tablecloths, and on each a small wicker basket holds cutlery, packets of salt and pepper, and the ever-necessary sachets of mayonnaise to put on your *frites*. The walls are alternately painted white or ox-blood red and the curtains match. You can see into the kitchen through an always-open hatch, where two cooks create dishes for the menu which, as far I am aware (and I've been going there regularly for ten years) is the same each week and very much of the rustic home-cooking kind: snails, mussels or charcuterie to start, turkey in cream sauce, steak, couscous or fried ham for the main course, plus the dish of the day, which is usually chicken or pork but occasionally *tête de veau*. I consider myself fairly adventurous when it comes to French cuisine – I'll try most things once – but I cannot bring myself to eat the boiled head of a calf, occasionally served with hairs still attached.

For dessert, there's always chocolate cake, lemon meringue pie and Madame the proprietor's rich, velvety crème brûlée, with its burnt sugar topping which cracks in an outstandingly satisfying manner when you hit it with your spoon (which is practically the law in France).

Feeling full and happy after the meal, we said our

goodbyes and headed off into the dark night to discover the lit-up valleys.

Illuminations are a way to celebrate the summer and local life, and they're held regularly in July and August. Sometimes it will be a single village that is 'illuminated' as part of an event like a concert or outdoor film screening. This particular 'illumination' involved driving from one participating village to another – more than a dozen of them in total. The involvement and output of each ranged from the wildly enthusiastic – where it seemed as though Christmas was taking place in the middle of summer, with gardens and houses lit up by fairy lights, spotlights and tea lights – to the less ardent, where the town hall, illuminated by blue, white and red lamps, was really the only indication that they were part of the festivities at all.

At the Moulin de la Course, where a mill has stood since 1340, flickering tea lights in little glasses highlighted the path to a huge courtyard, encircled by old stone buildings. Disco music was played as laser lights streaked through the air and bounced off the walls. A man in a straw boater danced with a woman in a floral tea dress, staring into her eyes and smiling. Children admired an old Vespa in a corner and their parents headed to a stall which sold mugs of cider and beer alongside freshly made crêpes plastered with chocolate spread.

In one small village, a woman stood proudly in the only clear patch in her tiny front garden, telling everyone that she had lit more than a thousand candles, which glowed alongside hundreds and hundreds of little garden gnomes, dolls, furry toys, plastic fruit, birds, sunflowers, butterflies, dogs and cats. Every inch of space was filled with an ornament of some kind and cars stopped outside her house, their passengers inexorably drawn towards the spirited display. Gnome-collecting is surprisingly popular in France. In the village of Gouvieux in Picardy, for instance, there is an elderly lady who has spent a lifetime collecting and repairing gnomes, and has over 2,000 of them in her garden.

Each village put on a show: in one, a small square hosted Benoît and Catherine, a pair of giants who danced to steel band music. Not real giants, of course – they are wicker-framed figures, and these two were visiting from the nearby town of Desvres, famous for its traditional pottery production. Benoît, who is around 3.5 metres tall, was 'born' in 1968, and Catherine came along a year later. These giants are a medieval tradition, and to this day, in these parts, they continue to be born, get married, have jumbo-sized babies (who are christened in grand public events) and die.

In yet another village, a cider press was in action and the air was filled with the intoxicating scent of freshly pressed apples. A crowd of enthusiastic tasters had gathered to try the fresh juice, but it wasn't as large as the group massing at the tent where last year's cider was being sampled. All the while, people staggered past carrying crates filled with bottles to take home.

In the next town, cars slowed down to admire hundreds of Christmas lights in a garden where a woman stood at the gate urging visitors to stop, park up and come in and buy waffles, which her husband was making, the sweet scent wending its way into open car windows. And, in the village of Beussent, famous for its chocolate factory, people queued up to buy chocolate at midnight – a rare treat in a land where all-day shopping is not yet normal.

Along normally deserted country roads, owls hooted under a starry sky as cows and sheep raised their sleepy heads, wondering what on earth was going on as a procession of cars passed by, trailing from one village to another until the early hours of the morning.

CHAPTER 4

The battle of the football coaches

'ARTHUR'S BACK — LOOK, up there, on the roof of the pigsty,' said Mark, as we tucked into our breakfast under a big umbrella in the courtyard and wondered if the rain would stop in time for the football match later that day.

Arf-an-ead Arthur, to give him his full name, is a large white-and-coral-coloured pigeon with peony-pink-tinged neck feathers. He'd arrived in our garden several months before with half of his head missing, having been either bitten off by an animal, or shot by a hunter's gun, leaving him bloodied and deformed. He wouldn't let us get close enough to try to take him to a vet, but he helped himself to food from the wild bird feeders, which I keep at the end of the dogs' part of the garden because they bark if any cats (who prey on the wild birds) appear, thus warning the birds to fly away to safety. Though Arthur shunned any help, he decided that my rotary washing line was a good place to recuperate and for most of the summer I had to put my washing out over a different rack so as not to disturb him. Over time his head healed up and he became tame enough that he would sometimes follow me into the chicken pens, sitting in the cherry tree in Tony Manero's pen. Tony is a lopsided Barbary duck with a strut (you can tell by the way he uses his walk he's a woman's man – no time to talk). Fat lot of good that swaggering would do him, though: all the girls had been removed from the pens because they breed like rabbits and had, in just one summer, produced fifty-two ducklings. We rehomed the girls but were stuck with the boys, who are not remotely like the cute Beatrix Potter characters you might think of, and they fight each other day and night in a most violent manner, using their claws to maim and injure their opponent. It meant we had to separate them into ones and twos.

'Why you don't just turn them all into duck à l'orange is beyond me,' Jean-Claude frequently said, licking his lips at the thought of it. 'They are the fattest, most enormous ducks I've ever seen. My Bernadette could turn them into a mouth-wateringly delectable meal. Washed down with a glass of Pinot Blanc, it would be a moment of perfection. I'm salivating at the thought of it. It would give their life meaning. That's what ducks are for, not for pampering and pandering to like you do. And a bit of roast pumpkin would be delicious with duck. Did I tell you I won the biggest pumpkin in the valleys contest? I did?'

Yes, he had told us – only about a hundred times, though Bernadette was less impressed. And I didn't doubt for one second that Bernadette's transformation of a bunch of pugnacious ducks to platefuls of tender meat covered in a sweet sauce would be unforgettable, but they would be the wrong kind of memories as far as I was concerned. It was, though, tempting at times, especially when it came to Tony Manero, who was the worst of the brawling bunch and had a pen to himself with the cockerels Ronnie and Reggie Kray. Inseparable twins, they seem to enjoy escaping from the pen whenever they want and then strut around the garden when they're not ganging up on the rest of the chickens. They nick the cats' food and chase the dogs. They fly up into the wild birds' food trays and scoff their seeds, and crow from the early hours of the morning through to the dead of night. They sit on the wall outside the kitchen waiting for me every morning and peck at the door of the pigsty for attention when I'm working.

Arthur had been absent for some weeks, but I could see that he was indeed squatting up on the pigsty roof, and Tigger, the cat-who-will-forever-be-a-kitten (a very energetic creature) was for once taking no notice of him. Instead, she and Fat Cat were crouched low, staying absolutely still, only their eyes moving as they watched the gravel path shake in front of the pigsty door. At first I thought perhaps it was a mini earthquake (we do get them occasionally, though they aren't particularly noticeable). We sat watching the ripples in the ground, until eventually a small pile of earth built up and the quivering, pink, pointy nose of a mole broke through. It was followed by whiskers on a head that appeared to have no eyes or ears, and a rather rotund body covered with brown velvety fur. Mark dived to rescue it before the cats could have their wicked way. It was the biggest mole we've ever seen, and it struggled wildly as Mark held it firm to stop it from escaping. He carried the creature down to the bottom of the garden and released it into the field where Thierry's cows live during the good weather. We watched in awe as it took just a few seconds for the mole's powerful paddle-like paws to dig into the soft soil before it was gone.

A couple of weeks later, we went to see Claudette to discuss tackling the laurel and elderflower trees that dominated the hedge between our gardens. One of my rookie mistakes when we had first come to France had been to plant a few sprigs, not realizing how tall they might become. Now fully grown and loving the fertile soil, they towered over the hedge, blocking out the morning sun in Claudette's garden and the afternoon sun in ours.

Jean-Claude was also visiting Claudette but, distracted, he was staring out of the kitchen window into the garden which he and Claudette look after together, growing vegetables and fruit for the whole family. He was frowning and muttering away to himself.

'*Merde* … that damn mole, he is tormenting me,' he said. 'He is digging bigger holes than ever before. He must be a giant – I've never seen such big holes. Do you have them too?' He asked us with hope in his eyes, since he always thinks that moles are singling out his garden.

'No,' we said truthfully, not daring to look at each other. 'We don't currently have any giant moles in our garden.'

Moles are Jean-Claude's pet hate. I often hear him cursing on the other side of the hedge. '*Putain*', '*Zut*', '*Sacrebleu.*' His head will appear over the top of a hawthorn bush: 'Those pesky moles – have they been in your garden as well?' Sometimes I say no just for the fun of it, though if he were to hop over the fence he'd see there are small molehills everywhere. This piques him a great deal; he feels he is being targeted by moles – it's personal. He asks Bread Man and Fish Man when they come to do their deliveries: 'How are the moles this month for you?' If they say not too bad, he replies, '*Merde.* They are all living in my garden.'

Now he believed he was being targeted by a giant mole.

'He'll be out there all day you know,' said Claudette as Jean-Claude grabbed an umbrella and dragged one of her firm-seated kitchen chairs out of the door. 'He'll be as happy as *un poisson dans l'eau*' (a fish in water) –

which was totally appropriate since it had started raining again. 'He never catches a mole, but he believes he will. He'll daydream out there, watch the wild birds, sniff the flowers and listen to the chickens clucking. Then he'll have a good reason to moan all day! Sometimes, it's the little things in life that make people happy.'

We promised Claudette that we'd cut the hedge the following week and waved goodbye to Jean-Claude through the window; he was seated in the middle of the garden, only his eyes moving as they scanned the ground, determined to find and obliterate the monster mole. But it was the day of the village football match and we didn't want to miss the kick-off, so we left him to it.

The steadily falling rain had done nothing to dampen the football fever that had gripped the village, and on our arrival at the *stade* we discovered that a small crowd had gathered. Jean-François had been training his fledgling team for a few weeks now. Each Tuesday night they jogged along the narrow winding roads of the village, sometimes followed by Thierry's dog, causing cats lazing under hedges to blink and stare as the squad of kids of assorted sizes and their puffing coach passed by, and setting off squawking chickens who were alarmed by the unusual human activity in the normally tranquil roads. They also had a weekly session at the new stadium and learned to play like a team.

Meanwhile, Jean-François' rival, Nico, a wine salesman from Hesdin who worked in the regional capital Arras, had also been coaching his players at our *stade* every week. Young, athletic and good-looking, he is what you might call a 'professional Frenchman', always immaculately manicured, coiffed, tanned, never without a pastel-coloured scarf tied elaborately around his neck (a skill that French people appear to be born with) and with just the right amount of stubble to look sexy instead of unkempt. The local fervour for football appeared to have inspired several mums in the village to turn out to watch him train his team – possibly more focused on the rival coach (and, by association, the opposition's progress) than watching their own kids run, jump and kick balls.

The match was 'just for fun' the mayor had said, but Jean-François apparently didn't hear that bit and took his duties seriously, putting the kids through their paces, determined not to let his nemesis win.

Hubert, the Parisian, was asked to referee the match on account of being a policeman; thus it was felt that he would stick to the rules (at least according to some). His physical fitness was also a bonus; although there had been a couple of other volunteers, there was some worry about them making it through to the end of the match without needing to take several breaks.

The mayor gave a speech and then, just after three o'clock, he blew the whistle for the match to begin. Kids aged between ten and fourteen ran about largely in disarray, but playing valiantly in the rain. About five minutes in, Thierry's dog Paco ran onto the pitch.

'He's good, let him play, he'll be the man of the match,' cried Jean-Claude, who had left his mole-watching duties to come and observe. Bernadette gave him a dig in the ribs.

It was 0-0 at half-time and the coaches rallied the kids with stirring speeches. The whistle blew for the start of the second half and almost immediately our side scored – sadly, though, it was an own goal, resulting from a failed attempt to pass to the goalie, who had been distracted by watching Paco run behind the goal in pursuit of a chicken that had escaped from Madame Jupe's garden.

The teams galloped up and down the pitch. Jean-François narrowed his eyes at Nico who grinned wolfishly; his team was winning. Not to be outdone, our side scored again and in the correct goal this time, which evened things up. The rain was coming down hard and thunder rumbled overhead. On the scoreboard, the chalk-scrawled numbers had all but washed away. The fugitive chicken ran squawking onto the pitch, followed by Paco. Distracted, the opposition team's goalie let a ball fly past him into the back of the net and two minutes later Hubert blew the whistle. The dog ran up to him, wagging his tail.

'Some people are on the pitch. They think it's all over … it is now,' said Mark, who never misses a chance to harp on about England's only World Cup win.

Against all the odds, it was a win for our village. Jean-

François beamed as the mayor clapped him on the back to cries of 'bravo' from the crowd.

There was a stampede for the *salle des fêtes* to get out of the rain. Once inside, the mayor thanked the boys and girls of both football teams for playing, the coaches for their efforts and everyone in the crowd for coming to support their communities. He kept it short, the puddles of water forming on the floor from our dripping coats spurring him on to allow us to hang them on hooks in the arcaded storage space outside. No one would dare move until he had finished: that is the way of French speeches, etiquette demands attention be given to the speaker. 'A *vin d'honneur* for the adults, pastries and juice and a big round of applause for the kids,' he concluded, and the room echoed to the sound of clapping and cheering.

Bread Man had dropped off a box of leftover pains au chocolat and croissants from the morning's stock for the kids to munch on. Croissants are a way of life in France, despite the fact that they are not actually French in origin. It's said that they began life in Austria as far back as the thirteenth century, where they were called *kipfel* (or *kipferl*) but they were more like bread. There's a legend that Austrian-born Queen Marie Antoinette hankered for a taste of home and her chefs made her a *kipfel* using puff pastry instead of dough – and so the croissant was born. Probably not true, but it might be!

These days, croissants are a breakfast staple to be dipped in coffee (you know you're pretty much French when you start doing that). There's even an annual contest for the best croissant-maker in every region. Bread Man, who delivers bread and pastries from the local boulangerie to the villages in the Seven Valleys where I live, has yet to become an official winner. But everyone here thinks he's the king of the croissants. When he opens the doors of his van, the scent of buttery croissants competes with the bouquet of just-baked baguettes. Resistance is futile.

For the past three years, I'd been teaching Bread Man to speak English. It started when his daughter wanted help with her homework and, though she has now left school and is away at a lycée boulangerie college in Normandy, learning the art of making bread, chocolate, ice cream and cakes so she can help her papa and one day take over the bakery, Bread Man still loves to chat in English. Unfailingly jolly, three times a week he toots the hooter in his little van outside my gate. He winds down the window, passes me a loaf of freshly baked bread, stops for a chat and tries to tempt me with cakes and pastries, sweet almondy madeleines, glossy tarte Tatin and irresistible cherry clafoutis.

I told him that there is an official National Croissant Day in America, which astonished him.

'*Non*, that's crazy, it ees croissant day every day,' he said, patting his ample tummy to emphasize the point.

'And my croissants are the best, I only ever make them with butter.'

'I thought all croissants were made with buttery puff pastry?'

'*Non*, all croissants are not equal – you must always ask for a *croissant au beurre* because they are made with real butter.'

Apparently, the *croissant ordinaire* (or *classique*) is made with margarine or vegetable oil, and generally is more crescent-shaped. It seemed like a good time to tell him about something else I'd recently learned to do with baking.

'I read on the internet that baguettes are long and thin because Napoléon Bonaparte had them made that way, so his soldiers could fit them down the legs of their trousers when they went into battle,' I said.

'What is zis, an English joke?'

'No, really. They had special long pockets on their trousers to hold the bread.'

'Ze truth is, nobody knows when bread began to be baked long and thin in France, but zey used to make baguettes up to two metres long in the old days.' He has trouble pronouncing 'th' sounds. 'Can you imagine me dropping off a baguette taller zan your Mark? But *non*, I don't believe Napoléon invented baguettes,' he said, shaking his head. '*Bah*, next you'll be telling me soup can be made from a stone!' He began laughing at his own joke, which referred to a famous folk tale about a hungry traveller persuading a number of villagers to donate various 'garnishes' (meat, vegetables and herbs) to a pot of boiling water containing a stone, which just needed a little help to bring out the flavours …

Bread Man held out a box of tarts to be admired. 'Pear crumble with speculoos.'

It's no wonder I am on a permanent diet these days.

'It's *magnifique*,' he declared, beaming at me. 'Madame Bernadette says this is the taste of autumn. And it goes very well with a cup of coffee …'

'Would you like a cup of coffee?' I asked him, though he rarely says yes as he has to dash from house to house and from village to village, dropping off all his delicious wares. But since he is a bit of a chatterbox, he's always late for the next customer.

'Another time,' he said, and then broke into a grin as he could see Tigger, the cat-who-will-always-be-a-kitten, swinging from a curtain in the window behind me.

'Okay, five minutes for a coffee,' he said, getting out of the van.

Bread Man, it turns out, is a cat whisperer. He came into the house, picked Tigger up and she went from bouncing off the walls to being a little angel with whiskers, who lay quietly, purring and stretching.

'Ow you say "*mignon*"?' he asked.

'Cute or sweet,' I replied.

'Ow you say zis?' he said, pointing to Tigger's oversized ears.

Ears is a surprisingly difficult word for a French person to say. I tried breaking down the sounds. 'Ee-ars' didn't work; he sounded like a donkey with a cold.

'My dad used to call them lugholes, when I was a kid,' I told Bread Man. My dad was a Cockney, native to East London. They have their own dialect and never pronounce the 'h' sound – think of Mary Poppins' chimney-sweep friend, Bert – and my dad liberally used Cockney slang when he talked.

'Lug'oles,' said Bread Man in the most perfect Cockney accent, dropping the 'h' flawlessly.

So if you ever meet a French Bread Man who looks like Super Mario in a beret and is able to speak English well enough to throw in a Cockney word now and again, you'll know where he learned it!

'Are you writing about me zis week?' he asked.

Apparently, a British couple holidaying several villages from mine asked him if he is '*the* Bread Man' who is mentioned in my weekly newsletters.

'*Oui,*' he said, '*c'est moi*, zat's me. I am ze best baker in ze norf.' Actually, I didn't write that he was the best baker in the north, but apparently I should have done. I have strict instructions from him to clarify the situation in this book.

His baguettes are the perfect partner to cheese. And on the subject of cheese, it's true to say that the French love it with a passion. They can't get enough of it. Supermarkets have entire rows filled with cheeses of all sorts: soft, hard, salty, creamy, blue, mouldy, ash-covered, sprinkled with herbs, mature, immature, bug-infested (Mimolette – that's you) and many more.

But Camembert occupies a special place in the hearts of the French people, and it's perfect with a baguette. Legend has it that one Marie Harel, born 28 April 1761 in Normandy, is responsible for the creation of this creamy, ivory-coloured cheese. A priest staying at a castle where she worked shared the recipe for Brie, a cheese made at a town nearby, with her. She modified the recipe and Camembert was born. It's probably not true – Camembert has most likely been around longer – but there definitely was a Marie Harel who made Camembert, so we're going along with this story. It's said that fifteen boxes of Camembert are sold every second in France!

Something else that holds the French enthralled are sausages or, more accurately, *andouillettes*. Every region in France seems to have its own version of *andouille* or *andouillette* (the difference being not just the spelling, but also the ingredients and how you eat them). *Andouilles* are usually bigger and eaten cold; *andouillettes* are boiled, generally eaten hot and they contain more bits of pigs' intestines – namely the colon – which gives a whole new flavour to the saying 'yum yum piggy's bum' (which is what I said to Mark as we walked home after he had tried *andouillettes* for the first and last time). We'd been invited to Monsieur and Madame Rohart's house and she had prepared these unique French delicacies to accompany some aperitifs. I hadn't actually explained to Mark what they were made from, and there was a chance that he might have enjoyed them; French people seem to go nuts for them. Besides, we had both tried *andouilles* before and Mark didn't mind them, so I thought perhaps he might not be averse to the more pungent *andouillette*.

In fact, we'd previously been to a festival dedicated to *andouilles* in the sleepy little town of Aire-sur-la-Lys on the border between the two departments of Nord and Pas-de-Calais. The Lys River, after which it is named, still runs through the town as it has for centuries, but it wasn't always so tranquil here. Thanks to its strategic position between the mountains of Flanders and hills of Artois, Aire-sur-la-Lys has been coveted and fought over, and has been, by turns, Spanish, Dutch and Burgundian. It wasn't until 1713 that it finally became French for good.

Visit the town on a Friday morning and you'll discover a vibrant little market occupying the cobblestoned Grand'Place under the watchful eye of the UNESCO-listed belfry, whose clock chimes every half an hour, surrounded by tall 18th century Flemish-style buildings. On one side of the square, the town hall is rather grand and its design and architecture is reminiscent of the Palace of Versailles. When Aire-sur-la-Lys finally became French under the Treaty of Utrecht, King Louis XIV granted permission for a new town hall to be built in 1716, but he imposed conditions

– it had to be in the French style. The architect was local: an ex-pupil of Jules Hardouin-Mansart, Louis XIV's chief architect who influenced the redesign of Versailles. You can't miss the pediment with its Sun God sculpture that represents the king, and symbolic fleur de lys carvings. The king wanted to make sure that the townspeople knew to whom they should be loyal, and the grand building was a brilliant reminder. In a corner of the squares, a former guardhouse built in 1600 and now occupied by the tourist office was funded by a tax on wine and beer (nothing changes, does it?), and is an incredible monument to the masons of days gone by, covered in friezes and sculptures (some of which depict shells – a nod to the fact that the town was on the pilgrim route from Canterbury to Santiago de Compostela). There's also what looks like a Romeo and Juliet balcony, but is actually a military verandah.

These days, the balcony plays host to the town bigwigs who, on the first weekend in September, toss foot-long *andouilles* that have been smoked over sawdust to the crowds gathered below. Get hit on the head with one of those and you'll know about it, but they do taste good.

The *andouillettes* that Madame Rohart was gently steaming were the colour of pink flesh and bore an uncanny resemblance to the appendage of a randy pig. She sliced one of the beasts open and out spilled a grisly assortment of innards, smelling just like a barn full of cows that had been kept in through winter. The stink wafted around our heads, filling our nostrils and curling its way down our throats.

I had tried them before in Troyes, which is famous for its *andouillettes*, and so I declined politely. Although this made Mark suspicious, he's got a lot more adventurous since we moved to France, so he took a slice and popped it in his mouth. How he didn't gag is beyond me: it was a heroic effort, and I apologize to anyone French reading this but, *non*, just *non*. It was good enough for Madame Rohart that he tried; French people are perfectly well aware that foreigners don't have sophisticated enough palates for this type of food. And it was enough for the rest of the guests – Jean-Claude, Petit Frère and Bruno, who lives two streets away from us – to slap him on the back and say '*bravo*'.

Bruno belongs to a thriving community of re-enactors – most are into dressing up as *poilus*, French soldiers of the First World War, or as medieval knights, but Bruno has a penchant for American GI uniforms, and when in costume he is apt to greet everyone he meets with '*allo birdy*' ('hello buddy').

He is an Elvis Presley fan, which may sound strange when almost every French person is a devotee of the French Elvis, Johnny Hallyday, but it's not quite as unusual as you might think. Until recently, there was a café in Dunkirk where the barman dressed as Elvis and customers were encouraged to share their passion and bring along their Elvis photos and records.

In fact, Bruno has an Elvis suit, which he wears for special occasions. Many mistake him for Johnny Hallyday, which drives him mad. '*Je suis* Elvis,' he says firmly, pulling his wig into place and his wide-buckled belt tight over his lanky frame, pushing back his glasses and smoothing down his non-Elvis-like dark bushy beard. His party piece is 'Jailhouse Rock'. As soon as he hears the iconic opening bars at any event (believe me, music of that era is still very popular here), he leaps up onto the dance floor and struts his stuff.

When he's not channelling Elvis, he's a farmer.

'I've got a proposition for you,' said Bruno to Mark. 'Jean-Claude tells me you have excellent apple trees in your garden and you've been wasting them on your chickens and apple pies …'

'A sacrilege,' interrupted Jean-Claude. 'They're super drinking apples …'

'Which leads me,' Bruno said, over the top of Jean-Claude, 'to ask you if you'd like to join the Cider Club.'

'Well, I like cider, but what's involved?' asked Mark.

'All of us here are in it. We take the apples from our gardens, plus any that are donated, get them pressed – there's a farmer up past the village of Hesmond that lets us use one of his mobile presses – then we mature the juice in Petit Frère's big barn, bottle it up and share it out. This year's batch will be good for next year, but we'll make sure you get some from our stash for this Christmas.'

Monsieur Rohart left the room and returned with a clear glass bottle filled with an amber-coloured liquid. He pulled out the stopper and poured everyone a glass.

'Nectar,' said Jean-Claude, wiping his mouth with his sleeve.

'My mother swears it keeps her young,' remarked Bernadette. 'She has a glass every day.'

'We're in,' I said, and Mark nodded.

'We'll let you know when we get things going again, but it will be next year as we're about done on this year's pressing,' explained Bruno.

After that, we were on a mission to taste cider so that we could learn more. We started that week at Le Douglas bar in Montreuil-sur-Mer, our nearest 'big town'. The fountain tinkled in front of the statue of Field Marshal Sir Douglas Haig, the commander-in-chief of the British Army who moved his headquarters to the town during the First World War. Kids were playing on the Place du Générale de Gaulle and dancing to the music of a Queen tribute band that was belting out toe-tapping numbers from a makeshift stage. I think that pretty much every town in France has a road or square named after the famous commander, as well as the writer Victor Hugo and Jean Jaurès, a prominent socialist leader from the late nineteenth/early twentieth century, who is still considered one of the main historical figures of the French Left. But not all French street names are quite so conventional: there's a rue Casse-Cul (meaning

Pain-in-the-Butt Street) in Montboucher-sur-Jabron; in Marseille there's a rue des Crottes, or Dog Turd Street; and in Pontpoint in Picardy there's a rue Pisseuse, which surely needs no translation.

The staff of Le Douglas weaved in and out of the tables that spilled out onto the square, deftly carrying trays laden with cocktails, glasses of wine and beer, and little bowls of nuts.

'If we ever get too old to chop wood for the fire and need to move to a town with more facilities, I could live here,' Mark said. It never occurred to us when we moved to France several years ago that one day we might find it a challenge to get up the stairs or keep a big garden under control. We're a long way off from that time just now, we hope, but it's something we have started to consider.

'We're not that old, we've got years to go yet,' I replied, smiling at him, and at that precise moment Mark popped a peanut into his mouth, bit down and broke a tooth, just like that. It could have been worse, though – my dad once broke his jaw eating a cheese sandwich.

The next day Mark was in agony. I phoned the nearest dentist, in a tiny village five minutes' drive away, where I was told that Mark would be 'seen to straight away'.

We headed off there and pulled up at 13 Grand Rue, which was the address I'd been given. It was a terraced house in a not very grand *rue*.

'You must have got it wrong,' said Mark.

'Nope, I asked three times to make sure,' I replied. I got out of the car, opened the gate to the pretty cottage-style property and made my way past the hydrangea bushes hanging over the path to the front door, where I saw a tiny brass plaque, hidden from the street, that read *Dentiste*.

I beckoned to Mark and pushed open the front door, as there was neither a bell nor a door knocker. It opened onto a hallway. A vase of flowers sat on a sideboard alongside china ornaments of ladies in crinolines. A row of closed doors featuring yellow glass panels cast a mellow glow over the hall.

'This isn't a dentist's surgery, it's someone's house,' whispered Mark. 'It doesn't even smell like it should.' He was right: a delicious aroma of garlic filled the air, strong and pungent.

I spotted the edge of a notice on the wall that was obscured by the open door. After shutting the door, I could see a sign displaying the word *Dentiste* and an arrow pointing up the stairs. At the top of the stairs were yet more closed doors, as well as one that was ajar, which led to a small room painted gingiva pink and containing a couple of rickety old white chairs. The walls were lined with posters of tooth decay in various hideous stages. All was silent.

We sat there waiting for several minutes. We heard the sound of a door opening downstairs and someone slowly mounting the stairs, huffing and puffing as they came closer.

A woman stuck her head round the door.

'Monsieur Marsh?' she asked, looking straight at me, which was a bit worrying.

'Mark is a little hard of hearing and his French is not as good as mine,' I explained, 'so can I come in too in case I'm needed to translate?' She beckoned us both to follow her into another room. It too was gum-coloured and sparsely furnished under harsh lighting, the sort that makes you look pale and unwell. There was a dentist's chair in one corner, over which a large lamp was positioned and a black rubber mask hung on a hook nearby. Next to the chair was a wheeled trolley on which lay an array of metallic dentistry tools. A couch, which Mark later joked was for patients who fainted, was pushed up against the window. There was also a small wooden desk covered in a mess of paperwork, along with a chair that Madame Dentiste invited me to sit on.

Mark sat in the dentist's chair and Madame pumped the pedal vigorously to lower it. She leaned in, he opened his mouth, she shook her head and tutted, sucked her teeth loudly and pushed her thick glasses back onto her nose before they fell off. She was speaking rapidly through her mask and I found it hard to understand her (Mark hadn't a clue what she was saying), but she made it clear that whatever had to be done had to be done immediately.

'She's going to sort it out now,' I said, 'and she wants to

know if you'd like something for the pain.' Mark nodded.

I can't tell you how glad I was that it wasn't me sitting there. Madame jabbed a needle into his gum and without waiting started energetically digging and drilling.

'Ouch,' said Mark. Madame carried on.

Mark rarely moans about pain. He once got thrown across the room by an electric shock. He'd been helping a friend with some rewiring at their *gîte*, and the electricity was, of course, turned off. But the friend's wife turned it back on without telling anyone so that she could boil a kettle for coffee, and Mark got a huge jolt. He rubbed his eyes a bit, then said, 'That hurt,' and got back to work.

Madame dug out three fillings, refilled them, and then filled the broken tooth. We never did understand what made her do work on the other teeth. We found a new dentist since then, though.

After this, the days began to get shorter. Some mornings started with a pale blonde sun struggling to break through a fog that was so low I felt sure I could take an empty jar, scoop it up, twist the lid on tight and keep a souvenir of autumn on my desk. The sun's rays filtered through the fog like blurry pastel-coloured fingers touching the bronze-edged leaves of the trees on top of a hill known locally as Mont Cauldron in the distance. Week by week, the air turned crisper and cooler, and the smoke from wood fires inside the houses carried on the wind. Autumn was upon us.

CHAPTER 5

The goat babysitter

IT WAS EARLY autumn, the time of year when the leaves of the hedges begin to turn gold, and spiders weave silky threads that glint in the sun between the lacy blooms of fool's parsley, a wild flower that grows in abundance along the edges of the fields. The air was crisp and cool, and the harvest was in progress, so some fields had been stripped down to bare earth, revealing rabbit runs and deer paths. But one morning, on our walk with the dogs, we came across an altogether more unexpected creature.

Screeching to a halt, Bruno the Labrador sniffed the air with more than his usual enthusiasm, Ella Fitzgerald – the spaniel who had turned into a German shepherd cross – stood stock-still in the middle of the road and stared ahead, and even Churchill, a diminutive German pinscher, looked up from his intense inspection of the gaps beneath the hedgerows. The dogs had, many years ago, unearthed a couple of baby chickens while rummaging under the hedges of Nine Owls Ridge. We call it this because some time ago, each morning for a whole magical month, nine owls would fly down from the trees where they were perched, observing the fields around them, and accompany us along part of the route. In truth this narrow country lane which runs between two hilly fields doesn't have an official name, like many of the roads around here, but has been known by the locals for several hundred years as 'the long road that leads to the farm of St Philibert' (which runs parallel to 'the short road that leads to the farm of St Philibert').

Ever since their exciting discovery, the dogs have continued to check every morning to see if they can find more chicks. On this particular day, there were none, but further along, as the path bends up to Hill Top Field (where Monsieur, one of the locals, keeps his white horses), a short-legged, shaggy-haired pygmy goat ambled along the road, dipping its head now and again to feast on the grassy verges. It took no notice whatsoever of the dogs, who ran up wagging their tails and heavily breathing a doggy hello. When we reached the goat, it gave us a rather dismissive glance and returned nonchalantly to its munching.

We guessed that the escapee probably belonged to a neighbour in the village who we know keeps goats. Sometimes, when I walk the dogs past his house, I can hear him in his garden behind a high wooden fence, sitting and chatting away to his pets as they gently bleat back.

'You stay with the goat while I go and tell the neighbour,' said Mark.

'Why do I have to stay with it? What if it bites me? What if it tries to run away? Those horns look a bit dodgy ...'

'You'll be fine. Just talk to it, and if it tries to wander off, stand in front of it – it's only little. I walk quicker than you. I'll be back quickly.'

And with that he turned back and disappeared from view as the road dropped into the village, the dogs bouncing along behind him. The goat watched them go and then slowly turned its head towards me. Its eyes locked on mine and its tufty white goatee quivered.

'I hope you're not going to play up,' I said. The goat made a sound like a cross between a snigger and a huff, as if I'd said something remarkably stupid. It started to amble along the side of the field in front of me. It was clear it was a boy.

'Stay there, stop walking,' I requested firmly, like I do when I'm trying to get the dogs to obey – which never works either. Mark says I am the lowest in the pecking order because I'm too soft with all the animals. The goat had rapidly come to the same opinion as the dogs, as it simply ignored me and sauntered off. I tried standing in front of him but I think he rather enjoyed the challenge, as he carried on walking straight ahead, not caring that his knobbly horns were digging into me as he pushed past. Finally, he found a patch of long grass that met his needs. He spread his front legs, tucked his head down and started to munch, occasionally lifting his head and looking at me as if to say: 'Are you still here?'

'Yum, nice grass, stay there, eat it all up, your owner will be here soon,' I crooned, hoping to soothe the goat and keep it from running off, while praying that Mark would come back quickly.

Thierry the farmer passed by in his tractor and slowed down when he saw me standing at the side of the road talking to a goat.

'Got a new friend?' he laughed as he leaned out of the cab to get a good look. The goat ignored him and began wandering off again. Thierry rolled his eyes and drove away, still chuckling. I trailed after the goat, begging it to stop.

Then Jean-Claude came by in his little white van, stopping to observe and pass comment.

'*Ah ah ah*,' he said (which is French for 'ha ha ha') when he saw me. 'I see you have found Gustave's goat. Be careful, he bites and butts.' He snorted with laughter: 'Why don't you let him find his own way home? He's a real devil, that one.'

'But what if he gets lost? What if he runs out in front of a car and gets hurt? I can't just leave him. Anyway, Mark will be back soon with Gustave – but if you see them, can you please tell them to hurry?'

'*Bah*. You know what they say, don't you? Just because trouble comes visiting, you don't have to take a walk with it!'

He shook his head and his laugh carried on the air as he drove off. I was pretty sure the tale of the goat-walking *Anglaise* would be doing the rounds within hours.

The goat's dark eyes were shiny against the patches of white around them on his wiry black head. By now we'd travelled quite a long way from the village, and I was starting to worry he might make a run for the forest, to which we were edging ever closer, and never be seen again. I remembered the dog lead in my pocket and managed to slip it over the goat's head while it was focused on a briar bush. The creature looked up and narrowed its eyes.

'Come on, you need to go home,' I said, and I gave a gentle tug on the lead. The goat complied. But only for a second – then it dipped its head to the grass again.

'I've got a roof to finish before winter comes. And a garage to build. And the chickens and ducks will be wondering where their breakfast is, and I have a million emails to deal with and a post to put on the website. Honestly, it would really help me out if you'd come with me.' To my surprise, the goat started walking alongside me on the lead. Every time I spoke to it in long sentences, the animal behaved. When I stopped or tried to get away with just a few words, he strayed off, dragging me along with him. If you happened to have been in the Seven Valleys on a lovely late summer morning, the sort of day when the warm blackberries were turning plump and juicy, and the farmers were smiling as they brought in that year's bumper crop, and you saw a small woman chatting non-stop to a goat on a lead – it was probably me.

I arrived back in the village just in time to see the door of Gustave's house opening and Mark emerging from behind it, followed by Gustave.

'Oh, you naughty boy, Casanova, what have you been up to?' Gustave, who is very tall, very pale and very thin, with long, black hair tied back in a ponytail and a dark goatee, slipped the dog lead off as he bent down to stroke the goat, which by now had become docile. 'Wandering off like that … your girlfriends have missed you.' The goat tried to eat Gustave's beard and bleated gently.

'Come in, come in, have another coffee.' I glared at Mark for having fun while I was cavorting with the disobedient goat across the valleys.

Gustave led us through the house and into the kitchen. The goat followed, stopping briefly to nibble a chair cushion before being taken out into the safety of the garden.

'I'm afraid I seem to have left the garden gate open,' Gustave explained as we sipped coffee in his kitchen, 'and Casanova, well, he's a bit of a character and the ladies love him you know, and I think he just wanted a little break from the attention.' We all looked out of the window where we could see the amorous goat living up to his name and chasing several females round a tree.

'One of my girls is expecting – would you like a goat?'

'Maybe,' I said, not daring to look at Mark, who I know thinks we have more than enough animals. Casanova started to headbutt the side of a tin shed, the sound echoing around the valley. Maybe not, I thought to myself.

As we said our goodbyes, Gustave asked if we might do him a favour.

'I have to go to a meeting in Lille in a couple of weeks' time and I'll need to stay overnight. Would you mind feeding the goats for me while I'm away? Casanova seems quite taken with you,' he said, grinning.

Of course, I said yes – what could possibly go wrong? But before then, I had my own journey to take.

Sometimes I feel like I live a double life. When I'm not cleaning up after animals, fighting the chickens for possession of the vegetable patch or getting to grips with the bureaucracy that is a constant of life here, I travel all over France, exploring every department. France is roughly the same size as the state of Texas. There are some 300 cities and around 37,000 communes (administrative areas that may encompass several towns), each with their own mayor. The landscape, weather and even the gastronomy can vary enormously from one department to another, so that you can sometimes feel that you've gone to a different country within a few hours of leaving one region and arriving in the next.

Every month I aim to visit one or two new areas, but even in my own region of Hauts-de-France, which includes the departments of Picardy, Pas-de-Calais and Nord, I constantly discover more places to love. So, when I was asked to appear in a film for the regional tourist office to showcase some of the wonderful local sites, I jumped at it. When they asked if Mark would join me, he wasn't at all sure about being on show – but when he was offered the use of a brand spanking new Harley-Davidson tourer bike for a week, he couldn't resist.

We'd barely got home from Gustave's house when the delivery lorry turned up with the bike.

'Hmmm,' said the driver as he eyed our gravelled path. 'It's a heavy bike – at almost 430 kilograms it weighs the same as a fully grown grizzly bear – stones don't suit it at all.' He scratched his head. 'I wouldn't ride it on that.'

He got it off the back of the trailer and left it on the road.

'We'll just leave it there,' Mark said. The driver was horrified.

'It will get stolen! It's a very valuable bike.'

'Nah,' Mark replied, 'this is rural France. People here leave their doors open all day.'

The sight of a shiny new Harley-Davidson bike in the village soon captured everyone's attention, and before we knew it we had a steady stream of visitors who wanted their photos taken sitting on it. It was fine for the more nimble villagers, but it took three of us to get Jean-Claude onto the bike and three of us to get him back down. The rumour spread that *les Anglais* were going to be film stars. It didn't take long to get out of control.

'Is it true,' asked Madame Bernadette, 'that you're going to be in a film with Gérard Depardieu? I really like him, do you think he'd come to tea if I was to make him a cake? Just you and Mark? Oh well, you never know what might come of it. Everyone has to start somewhere. But if you do meet him in the future, just remember to tell him I am his biggest fan, and I make exceedingly good cakes.'

And so it was that on a beautiful day, as marshmallow clouds floated across a Wedgwood-blue sky, we embarked on a bike ride beginning at the Opal Coast, both of us just about managing to squeeze into our old biker gear. When we'd first come to France, we'd dreamed of holidays on our motorcycle, but with so many animals to look after we gave up the dream and sold it – and a lot of cakes had been consumed since then.

The film crew followed us as we rode along the coastal road, the sea a luminous turquoise reminiscent of the Caribbean, past a Napoleonic fort and dunes dotted with pine trees. They swung out of the back of an open van, sent up a drone camera and yelled instructions at us. 'Turn round, come back, turn round again, stop looking directly at us – Janine, keep your eyes left, right ...' After a few hours we managed to get the hang of being filmed.

Basically, do exactly as you're told and never smile or wave at the cameraman.

Over the course of the next few days, we had the most glorious weather and not a drop of the rain we had feared. We visited Lille, where someone asked me for my autograph as we strolled up and down a cobbled street holding hands; clearly we were beginning to give off film-star vibes. Or perhaps, said Mark, my fame as a goat-whisperer had spread far and wide.

We spent a day at the Château de Chantilly, ogling the library which was bursting with historic books, and posing in the park. The flowers in their big stone pots wilted in the heat and so did we. We relaxed in the pretty hamlet created in the park in the mid-1770s surrounding the castle. The model village is said to be the inspiration for the hamlet that Marie Antoinette created at Versailles. Here we were to indulge in strawberries and the château's famous cream, which, it is claimed, was invented here by a chef called François Vatel. He worked for the owner of the castle, the Prince de Condé, who held a three-day party in honour of King Louis XIV in April 1671. Vatel was a perfectionist and had just fifteen days' notice to prepare lavish meals for hundreds of courtiers and their staff. Not everything went to plan. Apparently, not enough cream was delivered – so Vatel whipped it up with some sugar and vanilla and created Chantilly cream. Then, when too few fish were supplied to feed the vast number of guests, Vatel, distraught (and knackered after two weeks of non-stop preparation), fell on his own sword.

Actually, the cream story is probably a myth – but no one knows for sure. French history is full of such fables. 'Let them eat cake' was almost certainly not uttered by Queen Marie Antoinette when told that her starving subjects had no bread (it has been attributed to someone else, long before her reign). Napoléon has a reputation for being short, and had the nickname Le Petit Corporal, but at 5 feet 7 inches he was taller than your average eighteenth-century Frenchman. But why let the facts spoil a great story!

The head creamer at the Château de Chantilly (I'm not sure that's her official title) came out to mix the cream in front of the camera for the film.

'Can you do it again please, but this time look to the left as you do it?' asked the producer.

She did, mopping her brow.

And again, and again. The poor woman had muscles like Arnold Schwarzenegger by the end of it, whipping vanilla into cream until it was stiff enough to tip over our heads and stay in the bowl.

At the Thiepval Memorial, it became abundantly clear that I wasn't actress material, as I burst into tears at this most poignant monument to the lost of the First World War. Members of the crew were very kind about it, and even kept a clip of me snivelling in the film.

We travelled to the edge of the department, on the

border with Normandy, to Gerberoy, the village of roses, which has the official title *l'un des plus beaux villages de France* – 'one of the prettiest villages in France'. And in Amiens, we fell head over heels for the *hortillonnages*, the medieval floating gardens that lie in the shadow of the 800-year-old Gothic cathedral.

After a filmed visit to the Marquenterre bird reserve in the Bay of the Somme, we finished work just as the sun set over the calm waters of officially one of the most beautiful bays in the world. The sky darkened and filled with stars, and we stopped the bike at the side of the road, took off our crash helmets and gazed upwards, mesmerized. Sometimes when you live somewhere for long enough, you need to be reminded just how extraordinarily wonderful it is and why you went there in the first place.

By the end of the week I had become quite accustomed to being followed around by a camera crew and I posed with abandon. It was certainly less strenuous than renovating a house. After many years of laying concrete floors, plumbing, plastering and painting, replacing dozens of windows (some of them twice, on account of a monstrous hailstorm in 2016 which smashed the roof lights), we still weren't quite finished. We'd been putting off dealing with the kitchen extension, but winter was approaching and the time had come when it really had to take priority.

The extension was one of our first major structural

projects on the house, and we'd had no idea just how wet it can get in rural northern France. It hadn't occurred to us to study local building techniques; we'd built an extension when we lived in London, and that never had a problem. The kitchen of the house in France was long and narrow, like a galley. If Mark and I were in there at the same time, we bumped into each other as we passed. Half of the wall to the garden was in the form of a vast window that didn't open, and which turned out to be supporting the house structurally. I had nightmares that it would one day collapse, taking the house with it. So we took out the window, installed a lintel and extended out with a brick- and wood-built room featuring two very long roof lights.

For weeks, we boarded up the back of the house each night before we went to bed. We were more worried about wild pigs than burglars; my son Harry had come to stay with us to help with the building work, and as camping outside in a tent wasn't really very different from camping inside the house at that time, he decided to pitch up in the garden where he could see the stars at night. (Actually, he could have done that from inside the house if he'd slept upstairs, since the roof had gaping holes in it.) In the morning, he told us that he'd been woken in the dead of the night by the sound of growling, snuffling and snorting. Having watched too many horror films, he dreaded what he would find outside, but the noises continued and he knew that hiding inside a tent was no good against a werewolf. He gingerly pulled open the tent flaps and came face to face with a pair of close-set bloodshot eyes – and a whiskery snout. The pig was as surprised as he was and ran off, crashing through the hedge. After that, Harry stargazed from the loft.

The weather had been kind when we'd built the extension. The sun had shone and the brickwork had dried quickly, as had the glue on the felt-covered roof. We hoisted up the heavy roof lanterns, we put in the windows and laid a concrete floor. And then it rained. The water collected on the terrace that we'd built around the extension and seeped through the walls. We put a plastic roof up over the terrace and that cured the problem. But eventually, ten years of rain plus the destructive hailstorm took their toll. The exterior paint we'd used on the wood – the kind that came with a twenty-five-year guarantee – had long since failed to live up to its promise. The wood was rotting. And the terrace roof had begun to leak like a sieve.

Jean-Claude's advice, as he had sat watching us work ten years previously, was to cover the extension with metal sheets and a long overhang. 'It might look like a sheep shed, but it will withstand anything,' he'd said. We were relative novices then, keen on looks as much as practicality. It didn't take us long to realize that local advice trumps rookie ambitions. After that we would use metal sheeting on the roofs of all the outbuildings that we renovated.

It was disheartening to have to replace the roof, to remove all the rotting wood and felt, and cover it up with long-lasting cement board. But we set to, and the only interruption in a week of work was a day of rain and the job of looking after the goats.

When the time came, I wandered down the hill to Gustave's house in the lowest part of the village, which was drenched in mist and silent apart from Thierry the farmer's moth-eaten old dog Paco, who was patrolling the streets. He barked a greeting when he saw me. It's not his job to make rounds; he's supposed to stay at the gates of the farm, but he's at least ten years old and it's unlikely that he's ever had to guard the place against anything more than a rabbit that had lost its way or perhaps a cat daft enough to try to sneak past him.

My instructions were to give the seven goats fresh water and hay, and clear away any mess. Gustave said that his goats were used to being treated like dogs, albeit dogs that were disobedient, and that they liked to be talked to as it helped them to build trust. It should take around twenty minutes, he said, and usually his beloved pets were friendly and calm. I let myself into the back garden and Casanova and his harem ran bleating to greet me as I stepped through the gate.

It started off well. The goats sniffed and followed me about as I filled their trough with water. I chatted away to them as I pulled out the hay, then, as I bent down to pick it up, one of them jumped on my back. I stood abruptly and it fell off. I stooped again and once more the goat jumped on my back and another one followed. They took turns to leap on me. I trod in goat poo. I'll be honest, any dreams I'd had of owning goats of my own withered and went the way of the pigs I'd hankered after. Hogs eat you out of house and home, and the amount of poo that needs to be shovelled up every day is hard to believe. For years I had yearned to have more animals – a sort of Noah's ark of farm animals was my fantasy – sheep were on the list too, and even a couple of cows. But the reality of animal husbandry is hard to avoid when you live in a farming village. The dream gave way to common sense – no, I probably didn't have time to milk a cow, and what would I do with the milk? Shearing sheep takes time and money. It's probably more worthwhile if you're prepared to eat your animals, but I have accepted that's never going to happen; I fall in love with them all. And right now, it was clear that these goats, cute as they were, were going to be hard work. They butted me, they climbed on me, they took no notice of my requests to behave. One of them even spat at me. And they shouted, sounding like a bunch of angry children.

I persevered. They knocked everything over and Casanova banged his head against the side of the shed as if he were rallying the troops to attack. The girls tried to eat my camera bag.

Eventually, Mark came to rescue me as I'd been gone

so long. The moment he appeared the goats were docile and well behaved. He pulled the straw from my hair, helped me clean my shoes, wiped the mud from my face and said tenderly: 'No, we are not getting goats.'

We left to go home, and on the walk down the shady *chemin* that runs alongside Gustave's house, we came across a curious thing. Walnut shells were scattered along the footpath. Like a nutty Hansel and Gretel trail, it led from the walnut tree outside the Parisians' house to Jean-Claude's barn a little further along, where we spotted him sitting in his little white van, which was parked in the mud.

'*Bonjour*,' we said as the dogs bounced about excitedly – they like Jean-Claude a lot.

'Mffmmmfff,' he replied. He was busy munching away on walnuts like a giant squirrel. 'I'm on a diet ... it's been so hard, I'm starving, I don't think I can carry on like this.'

We commiserated and asked him how long this had been going on for.

'Four hours,' he revealed, looking pained.

Bernadette had told him in no uncertain terms that he must cut back on his calorie intake. It can be easy to overdo it where we live. Despite being in the middle of nowhere, in the Seven Valleys there's always plenty of temptation. Aside from deliveries to the village, local towns are not that far away by car and are full of fromageries, boulangeries, patisseries, charcuteries, farm shops, markets, wine *caves* and chocolateries. But since Bernadette had issued her edict, Jean-Claude knew that she would be asking the people who work in the shops if he had been in. I promise you, despite rumours to the contrary, not all French people are thin!

But foraging, he argued, is surely allowed; it's almost the law in France. And besides, no one could see him eating the walnuts. Except us.

He got out of the van to shake hands with Mark and kiss me on the cheek, a maroon felt hat sat over his ruddy face. 'It's Bernadette's,' he mumbled. 'She bought it in Avignon in 1981 when we went on holiday there. I have to wear it because she cut my hair too short and my head is cold.' He snorted with disgust and removed it to show us how his usual unruly mop had been shorn.

'Claudette asked me to ask you if you'd like a cockerel. She's getting rid of some of her birds.'

'No, thanks,' I said. 'I've got more than enough of the buggers in my garden already.'

'No, it's for eating. She'll kill it and I'll bring it round later.'

I thanked him but declined, as we'd learned our lesson with trying to get to grips with plucking a chicken once before: it's hard work and not remotely pleasant. Plus, I had visions of scenes from a horror film, as had happened to a British friend who lives in a gorgeous little bungalow on an island in the middle of the river in Saint-Omer.

To get to her house, you have to pull yourself across on a boat, which is moored to the side of the river and connected to the island by a chain which you must tug on to go back and forth. The hall of the property is lined with magnificent wood panelling, which the man who built the house in 1902 installed after buying it from a mansion that was being renovated in Paris. In the garden is a three-room summer house built by American soldiers in the 1940s when they were billeted in the area.

My friend is animal mad. She once drove to Bosnia to rescue a dog and she has a three-legged cat. She keeps a TV on the terrace for her chickens, whom she is quite sure love to watch it, and she will often sit there watching TV shows with the birds on her lap.

She told me that one of her French neighbours, who lived on another island a little further along, knocked at the door one day and asked: 'Do you like *coq*?'

'Oh yes, coq au vin is one of my favourite dishes,' she replied, fervently hoping that the neighbour couldn't hear her husband sniggering in the kitchen.

'Ah good,' said he, 'I have a *coq* for you.' And he handed her a dead cockerel for the cooking pot. It had one eye hanging out, its neck was flopped over and it lay there as still as death.

My friend thanked him and off he went, pulling himself back across the river. She then headed into the kitchen to show her husband the neighbour's gift. Like me, she doesn't kill her birds, just eats the eggs they lay, so she was a bit taken aback at having a deceased cockerel thrust into her hands.

The pair were stood looking at the poor departed creature when suddenly the eye that was still in its socket opened, the neck straightened up a little and the bird gave a feeble squawk and sighed. They fed and watered him and stayed up all night to watch over their one-eyed patient. Against the odds he survived, and they named him Marcel.

Marcel the one-eyed cockerel lived in safety on their island for many years with his wonky neck, hiding whenever anyone came out to the garden who wasn't my friend or her husband, which you can't really blame him for. Eventually, he died at a ripe old age after living a long and happy life.

'I don't suppose you want to go hunting at the weekend, do you?' Jean-Claude asked Mark.

'It's not my thing really,' replied Mark. We understand that it's a way of life here, but it's not our idea of fun. We'd been to Jean-Claude's 'hunting lodge' a couple of times, but only for social occasions. It's in a German Second World War bunker in the woods and no time has been wasted on trying to enhance its looks: it's very much a 'man cave', with the barest of necessities. Accessed by a metal door, there are no windows and the murky interior is somewhat grim and damp. Lit by oil lamps, the building's concrete walls seem to absorb the light, but as your eyes adjust you see a table covered with an incongruously chintzy plastic tablecloth and some chairs that have seen better days. The hunters hunker down in the bunker to play cards on days when it's so wet or cold that no one can really be bothered to stalk through the woods in pursuit of small or harmless animals. There's a two-ring gas burner, an assortment of pots and pans purloined from Bernadette's kitchen cupboards, and an old bookshelf unit filled with cups, glasses, plates, a box of cutlery, board games and packs of cards.

'*Merde*,' said Jean-Claude. 'I'll have to go with that idiot Gaétan, as my usual partner Baptiste has pulled out because of *bom-bee*.'

'What's *bom-bee*?' Mark whispered to me, as my French is better than his.

'No idea,' I replied. 'Jean-Claude, what is *bom-bee*?'

He held his hands up over his head making the V-sign with his fingers, 'You know, *bom-bee*.'

He looked madder than ever, dressed as always in hunting greens, wriggling two fingers in a V-sign just above his eyes.

'Baptiste says his children begged him to give up the hunting because they didn't want him to kill *bom-bee*. Like I keep saying, you should never give an animal a name. His kids love that film and now he says he feels guilty and he won't come hunting anymore.'

'Oh Bambi, he means Bambi,' realized Mark.

'It's just not my week,' said Jean-Claude. 'This *bom-bee* thing is daft and Gaétan is okay, but he drives me mad with his chain-smoking – the animals can smell him a mile off. We'll catch nothing to put in the freezer. It's just one more problem what with Bernadette being home all the time now she's retired. It's making everything difficult.'

She had, he said, informed him that he was to grow sensible vegetables like lettuces, cabbages, onions and carrots, and to cut back on the pumpkins. Jean-Claude was not happy about this at all. He has always lavished love and tender care on his pumpkins. Not because he likes to eat them, as he gives most of them away, but because he loves to enter pumpkin-growing competitions. For several years running, he held the 'Biggest Pumpkin of the Valleys' title, but in the last two years he had lost out to a usurper from another village. Jean-Claude was determined to stage a comeback, but Bernadette was putting a damper on his grand plans.

'I'm not a quitter though,' said Jean-Claude. 'It's not *la fin des haricots* ...' (which doesn't have anything to do with haricot beans, but in this context means 'all is not lost').

He told us he had a cunning plan. At the bottom of the garden, where Jean-Claude leaves some nettles to grow to encourage the bees and where Bernadette rarely ventures, he has a pumpkin patch quietly thriving.

CHAPTER 6

Friendship doesn't freeze in winter

A WEEK BEFORE Christmas, the mayor switched on a single string of twinkling white lights outside the town hall. Madame Bernadette put up a life-size plastic inflatable Santa Claus (when I say life-size, you know what I mean – I haven't actually met him in real life). It dangled from the gutter of her farmhouse roof, forlorn-looking for the most part but swinging about wildly when it was gusty, seeming to wave to all who passed by. It's not that we don't do Christmas here in the sticks, it's just that it's generally a low-key affair and most of the action takes place behind tightly closed shutters which guard against the cold wind that swooshes through the valley.

Bread Man was doing his deliveries sporting a Father Christmas hat instead of his usual blue workman's cap or black beret. Jean-Claude was working on his *bûche de Noël* skills by making a traditional French Christmas log cake. According to Bernadette, he once made an exotic mango and raspberry concoction with a sweet Chantilly cream filling that was so good it would please Curnonsky. This is the ultimate accolade when it comes to food because Maurice Edmond Sailland, known by his pen-name of Curnonsky, was regarded as the 'Prince of Gastronomy' in France. Born in Angers in 1872, at eighteen he set out to be a writer – but his passion in life was food. Putting the two together he became the most celebrated authority on French cuisine in the twentieth century. His recommendation could make a restaurant's fortunes. He would travel from his Paris home, taking journeys lasting many hours, to enjoy a single dish in the south of France and then drive straight back to Paris. If Curnonsky liked it, you knew it had to be good.

People in these parts talk about recipes like the rest of us talk about the weather. 'Did you see that Chef so-and-so has created a new macaron flavour? What did you think about the recipe for slow-roasted celeriac with black truffle butter in such-and-such magazine?' People discuss whether a famous Michelin three-star chef might have been better to use this ingredient or that. And they are serious. Everyone is a gourmand in France, it seems.

There are thousands of French food blogs. It's said that two cookery books are published in France every day. Recipe books have been popular for centuries here; the great writer Alexandre Dumas, famous outside of

France for *The Three Musketeers* and *The Count of Monte Cristo*, is just as well known in his country of birth for his food writing as his novels, and he himself said that his masterwork would be on the subject of culinary history. Indeed, the last book he wrote was a 1,150-page manuscript about the history of food that was filled with recipes, including fifty-six ways to dress an egg, thirty-one ways to treat a carp and how to flavour food with ambergris (a secretion from a sperm whale's digestive system).

Family recipes are passed down through generations and food is prepared with love and reverence. Whenever Claudette makes *carbonnade Flamande*, a beef-and-onion stew flavoured with beer and sugar, she tops it with slices of mustard-slathered gingerbread in the traditional way, which she says reminds her of being a child. It is the exact same recipe that her mother cooked on a chilly Sunday morning, leaving it in the oven while the family went to church, so that when they came home ready for lunch the house was filled with the comforting aroma of the casserole and just a hint of spices from the gingerbread.

From home cooking to haute cuisine, the French take pride in it all. When I was once invited to review a Michelin three-star restaurant, the chef came out to welcome me when I arrived and told me that he would be preparing a special treat for me: twelve courses, a taste of everything on the menu that night.

'Twelve courses!' I heard myself exclaim in shock.

'Madame Marsh. It may sound a lot, but you must think of it as follows: if the Queen of England were to arrive unexpectedly, one would make room for her, and it is so with my dishes – you will make room.'

And of course, I did. In case you think that I made a total glutton of myself, the portions were quite small. They were also very French. The first course was a bowl of steak tartare, which is much admired in France – minced raw beef. It was combined with a chopped raw oyster drizzled with zesty sherry vinegar and fragrant olive oil. I failed the Frenchness test, though, as I couldn't manage to eat it. I did try a morsel, because it's my job to write about my experiences, but quite honestly I'd rather eat grass.

'Madame doesn't like it?' asked the waiter, in a tone that implied I might just have broken his heart. Fortunately, I redeemed myself by demolishing the next eleven courses.

It could have been worse. Dumas once told the tale of a true gourmand, a viscount who took precisely one hour and fourteen minutes for a lunch at which he was served 288 oysters, a soup made of swallows' nests, steak and potatoes, trout from Lake Geneva, truffled pheasant, partridge, asparagus, peas, bananas, strawberries, two half-bottles of Johannisberger wine, two bottles of Bordeaux, half a bottle of sweet white wine, half a bottle of sherry, coffee and liqueurs. He consumed the lot.

Though you will often read that all French women

are slim, and there are plenty of books on the topic guaranteed to make you feel totally inadequate, it's really not the case in real life. *Les femmes françaises* are perfectly normal and all different sizes, though it is true that those from Paris are often stick-thin. That's partly due to walking a lot (apparently the average person in the French capital covers a distance of 6 kilometres a day on foot), but also it's a 'thing' in Paris. I once witnessed a slender Parisienne order a bowl of lettuce at the Café de la Paix near the Paris Opera House and she nibbled delicately on each leaf while her companion made his way with relish through three generously proportioned courses. You may ask how I knew she was a Parisienne. Well, apart from being wafer-thin, she was dressed all in black (it is a fact that Parisians only wear dark colours – bright colours are for the provinces) and she critiqued the clothes of women passing by without trying to hide it.

If French people are not talking about food, they're shopping for it, planning to cook it or eating it. Food is on everyone's lips. It pops up in everyday conversation even when not talking about food. In French, the phrase for 'making a fuss', for instance, is *'en faire tout un fromage'* (literally, 'to make a whole cheese out of it'). Which can be very confusing if you're shopping for cheese, can't find what you want, sulk about it and then your French friend tells you not to make a fuss.

At Christmas, the preparation of food moves to

another level still. There is the sharing of recipes and the whereabouts of favoured cheese-makers, wine cellars, patisseries and boulangeries, where to source the best smoked salmon (Perard in Le Touquet – we are all agreed), and the posting of photos of *bûches de Noël*, gingerbread loaves and cocktails online. There is an old saying that 'cooking is love made visible' and in France it's something that is taken to heart.

I had three guests in the house that particular Christmas: baby cockerels (not running wild, of course, I'm not quite that far gone – they were in a cage). They arrived at a time when chickens aren't normally born, but the end of the year was unseasonably warm – even the roses had carried on blooming into early December. Almost as if nature had planned to play a trick, as soon as the baby birds hatched, the weather became treacherous: a dense frost fell and Barbra Streisand, their not very maternal mother whose squawks sound as though she is singing 'I am a woman in love', lost all interest in her offspring. We had no choice but to adopt them, as they had no chance of surviving the cold. Barbra Streisand was not remotely bothered by their disappearance and went straight back to strutting and screeching her signature tune.

Bread Man, who is still not quite sure whether I keep pigs hidden in the house, due to a language misunderstanding over the fact that my office is in the former pigsty, raised his eyebrows when he popped in to warm up and saw Genghis Khan, Charlemagne and Napoléon throwing themselves at the side of the cage like tiny dinosaurs.

As we sat in the kitchen with our coffee, I could see Bread Man's eyes darting about. No doubt he was looking for the non-existent pigs. All I needed was the septic tank to explode again, as it did the day we moved here, which led to me being named Madame Merde by my neighbours, and Bread Man would have a story to dine out on for the rest of his life.

Along with my usual baguette, he had brought with him a local, traditional Christmas cake called a *coquille du Nord*, which has been made in the far north of France since at least the sixteenth century. They're not for the faint-hearted: picture a large, sweet brioche bun filled with butter, sugar and raisins – and yes, just looking at one makes you put on weight.

We shared the brioche and chatted about Christmas traditions. His kids leave wooden clogs under the tree for Santa to put gifts in, while my kids have sack-like stockings. His family enjoy their main meal on Christmas Eve and it can go on for six hours. The *bûche de Noël* is a must. We eat ours on Christmas Day and we set fire to brandy poured over a Christmas pudding. That made him laugh.

I told him about the British custom of sweet mincemeat pies that are made from dried fruits, not meat as the name might suggest. It's a tradition that's been popular since the Middle Ages, when it was believed that the little pies would bring good luck for the coming year.

That stopped him in his tracks. 'A cake of good luck ... *dac dac dac.*' He sounded a bit like a demented duck when he said this. It's a sound that French people make when they're thinking things through or reaching the end of something, like a thought process. Nobody French seems to be aware that they actually make this noise and if you tell them that they just *dac*'d they will either look surprised and laugh or deny it.

The French are a superstitious bunch. They have numerous baffling beliefs about food bringing luck – either good or bad. For instance, you should never place a baguette upside down on a table because it invites famine into your house. Apparently, this superstition originated in the days when executioners could take things from shops without paying and bakers would leave bread upside down for them. You should also never have thirteen people at the dinner table in France; it is sure to bring an ill wind, they say. Perhaps this belief comes from the Last Supper where one of thirteen diners, Judas Iscariot, turned traitor. If there are thirteen individuals around a table in a restaurant in France, a waiter may place an egg on the table to mark a fourteenth dinner guest.

And if you clink glasses together before enjoying a glass of wine, you must look each other in the eye or you risk being unlucky in love for seven years. Some say that this habit dates back many centuries, and was a safeguard against being poisoned: a robust clinking would cause some liquid to spill over the edges from one glass to the other, and by making eye contact, the two drinkers offered reassurance to each other that there was no reason to pay particular attention to the glasses.

If you want good luck, Jean-Claude assures me that all you need to do is twiddle the red pom-pom on a French sailor's bonnet. I once saw three sailors standing outside a bar just off the Champs-Élysées in Paris, drinking glasses of pastis on a sunny day, and I stood watching for ages to see if anyone would go up to them to ask if they could wobble the bobble. Nothing. I was very disappointed.

'I like this cake of good luck,' said Bread Man. He had a gleam in his eyes, especially when I told him that some people believe that the more of these little cakes you eat, the more luck you get.

'Could you give me the recipe when I pop by next week? I might have a go.' I think it is entirely possible that should you ever come to France and be unexpectedly offered a mince pie at Christmas, you may thank me for starting the trend.

The weather continued to get colder. The day before Christmas Eve, I got up, turned on the tap and nothing came out. The pipes had frozen. Despite insulating as if we live in the glacial Arctic, there was one spot in the house, in a far corner of the roof, that we hadn't been able to reach because of the deep slope, and we were sure that this must be at the root of the icy problem.

Mark climbed onto the ice-stricken roof, removed the tiles and cut through the roof covering. Meanwhile, I plugged my hairdryer into a long extension lead and passed it up to Mark, who aimed it at the pipes. It was only a matter of time before someone would pass by to witness a tall Englishman dressed like a yeti hair-drying the roof of an old farmhouse.

The sound of Thierry's tractor coming down the hill made Mark roll his eyes and groan. Thierry didn't stop, but lifted a hand in greeting and furrowed his brow in confusion.

'I think we might get away with just saying it's a loose tile,' called Mark. But a couple of minutes later, we heard Jean-Claude's van approaching from the bottom of the hill. Despite it being new, a replacement for the old spluttering, smoking van he used to have which was destroyed in the 2016 hailstorm, he's the only person we know who drives around the village at 15 kilometres an hour and the sound is distinctive. Jean-Claude peered through the window of the van and decided it was worth braving the cold to get a closer look.

'*Il fait un froid de canard*,' he announced, rubbing his hands together. How on earth can it be as cold as a duck? Sometimes I think I'm getting the hang of the French language and then I realize I'm not getting it at all.

'Blow-drying your house, then? Have you run out of wood again?'

He was referring to our first winter here, the coldest for decades, when running out of wood almost caused us to give up the good life before it had even started and go back to London. But we are wise to it now and stock up years in advance, partly with supplies from the Wood Man, Monsieur Lagasse, and partly from Mark being a member of the local Wood Club, a group that manages the trees in the fields and forests owned by Claudette in return for a stash of the wood.

'D'you want a drop of something to help?' called out Jean-Claude, pulling a small silver flask from his pocket. 'It's a Christmas present from my uncle who lives in the Ardèche. Home-made hooch. You can't drink it, it's foul, but I reckon if you pour it over the pipes it will thaw them out. I've been using it to clean the mould off my tools – it works a treat. He's staying for Christmas. Come and meet him – aperitifs at our place tonight.'

'I don't know about the pipes, but I think that Mark might need something to defrost him when he comes down.'

'Don't drink this stuff, whatever you do,' he shuddered. 'Just pour it over his frozen bits.'

Of course, the tale was soon doing the rounds: 'The only *Anglais* in the village are blow-drying their house. Yes, really, he's sliding about in the bone-shattering, teeth-chattering cold on the roof with a hairdryer and she's at the bottom of a ladder, dressed like she's off to climb Mount Everest ...'

After what seemed like an age out there in the frozen air, the water started flowing, but not before an unusually large number of neighbours had passed by to stop and stare. We hastily covered the pipes with thick foam sleeves, thrust as much insulation as we could into the space, re-covered the roof and put the tiles back on.

In the cold months, when we're not doing our normal day jobs, we spend time working on the house's interior, making furniture, cupboards, tables, wardrobes and shelf units, and completing decorating jobs. Before we came to France, Mark had taken several courses to make sure we had built up the skills to renovate the house ourselves. A few days spent learning brick-building, roofing, plastering, plumbing and tiling had meant that we didn't need any outside help. At the start of the project, we certainly weren't experts, but YouTube tutorials helped to fill in any gaps from the courses, and with all the big jobs out of the way, we were steadily working through each room to create furnishings based on photos in magazines or items I'd spotted on the internet. After sorting the pipes out, we spent the afternoon in the workshop, making a set of wardrobe doors for our bedroom, before heading down the hill to say hello to Jean-Claude's uncle.

Generally speaking, our neighbours discourage the bringing of bottles of wine or alcohol when you go visiting, but, having been warned about the mould-cleaning moonshine, I grabbed a bottle of Armagnac flavoured with orange that I'd brought back from a recent visit to the Gers region in south-west France, which used to be part of the area known by the ancient name of Gascony. It's a corner of the country that feels like the land that time forgot. You'd better take trousers with an elasticated waist with you if you go to the Gers, since they *love* their food there – perhaps more than any other region I've been to. I went there with my friend Lucy and, though I am pretty sure I can't be tempted to leave northern France, if I did, the Gers would be a contender.

There are no motorways in the Gers. Not one. In fact, there's very little public transport. And there's no mass tourism. The Gers is bucolic, beautiful and bubbling with bonhomie. It's where Armagnac, France's oldest *eau de vie*, is made. And, like everything to do with the Gers, the spirit is not mass-produced but made by artisans, family-run businesses and small domaines. At the end of November through to December, some of the Armagnac-makers open their cellars up and hold an *alambic* party (the word is said to be derived from the Arabic *al-'anbiq* meaning 'the still' and from the ancient Greek word *ambix*, meaning 'cup [or 'cap'] of a still') to mark the start of the distillation process. Being mostly small producers, the still (a sort of back-to-the-future, nutty-professor-type steam engine crossed with a Willy Wonka Chocolate Factory machine) is hired for a few days rather than each producer owning one. Topped with copper funnels, a labyrinth of pipes lead to bowls and taps. The rented still goes from cellar to cellar, tended to by experts who work shifts through the day and night to manage the process, feeding the flames with gnarly old vines.

Down a nameless, narrow, winding country lane under a frosty star-filled night, Lucy and I eventually found our way to the Château de Millet near the town of Eauze, where an *alambic* party was to take place. The cellar was toasty thanks to the heat from the still, and a live band played jaunty jazz Manouche. Locals and strangers sat side by side on benches at long tables, and were served bowls of hearty *garbure*, a local soup that is more like a stew made from cabbage, garlic, vegetables, white beans and amber-coloured duck confit, followed by generous portions of braised pork and potatoes, all mopped up with chunks of crusty baguette, and followed by some Gascony apple pie laced with Armagnac. The château's wines flowed, and we also drank pure Armagnac that trickled from a pipe straight from the hissing hot still. It takes your breath away, I can tell you.

Clutching the bottle of Armagnac, I knocked at the door to Jean-Claude and Bernadette's house, which opens straight into their small sitting room, and we were ushered in, out of the cold. They have managed to cram in a sofa, three armchairs, a dining table and four chairs, two long wooden sideboards and a huge wood fire. The stuffed head of a long-dead deer stares down in a rather disapproving way and ornaments cover every surface.

The room was swelteringly hot, so my glasses steamed up immediately.

We were introduced to Jean-Claude's uncle Thibault, who was short and stocky like his nephew. Sat before the fire, his shiny bald head reflected the flames, while a baggy and wrinkled suit matched his baggy eyes and wrinkled skin.

'I was just saying to Jean-Claude that all I need for Christmas is a pretty English lady and he brings me you,' he remarked. He stood up and smiled, his grin revealing more than a few gaps in his teeth. Pulling my right hand towards him, he dropped a noisy kiss on it. 'I am alone – my girlfriend left me, you see.'

'Uncle,' said Jean-Claude, 'behave yourself.'

'When you kiss a rose, you will always have blood on your lips,' Thibault replied, mournfully.

Bernadette came into the room. 'Amandine didn't leave you, she had to stay behind and look after her *maman*. And she has phoned you seventeen times in two days.'

'Ah yes, but if she really loved me she would have come with me,' he sighed, though he had a smile on his face. 'You must have some of my rum. I made it myself. It is the taste of Christmas – I put spice in it for a special flavour.'

'Uncle, Janine and Mark have brought some orange Armagnac, so let's save your rum for later.' Bernadette beckoned to me to follow her into the kitchen.

'For heaven's sake, don't drink his rum – you will miss Christmas if you do and most likely have to go to the doctor. We keep telling him how much we like it and then we pour it over the fence at the bottom of the garden as fast as we can to get rid of it ... He seems to have an endless store of it hidden away. I don't dare pour it down the sink in case it blows up the septic tank and I can't tip it down the drain – I don't want it to get into the water supply.'

She pulled some tall glasses out of a cupboard and took a bottle of sparkling wine from the fridge.

'He's driven down from the Ardèche because his girlfriend Amandine asked us to invite him so that she doesn't have to worry about him as well her sick mother, but *mon Dieu*, it's going to be a challenging Christmas. He is a serial flirt. Personally, I find him a little irritating, but he seems to be irresistible to women – all of my girlfriends adore him. He has been married – and divorced – four times. You would think that at the age of seventy-two that he would be better behaved but *non*, he is as frisky as a rabbit.' She arched her eyebrows and shook her head.

We returned to the sitting room where Thibault was regaling Mark and Jean-Claude with stories of his past.

'I once dated Brigitte Bardot after I met her in a lift in an apartment block in Paris ...' He stopped to allow us to be impressed by this revelation. Jean-Claude, sitting behind him, winked at me.

'She was so beautiful – older than me, of course. But it was never going to work out for us. I like a peaceful life: I am a poet. She liked the fast life in those days … we'd probably get on now she's quietened down a bit. Maybe if Amandine doesn't want me, I should get in touch with Brigitte.'

He sipped his drink, turned his eyes towards me and said, 'You look a little like Brigitte when she was younger, you know.'

I nearly spat my drink out trying not to laugh, but Mark made no such attempt and guffawed, loudly. I look nothing like Brigitte Bardot except that we both have two arms, two legs and a head. Bernadette and Jean-Claude said they had to go and start preparing dinner. I could hear their sniggers from the kitchen.

Thibault spoke a bit of English when they were gone. He was a writer and former radio and TV presenter, and had spent time in Britain in the 1970s interviewing Second World War veterans for a radio series. He told us that he 'loved British ladies, they are so repressed, so ripe for seduction'. Neither Mark nor I knew how to answer that one – it wasn't really necessary, though, as Thibault was quite happy to talk without requiring any feedback.

'I am a poet of the melancholy type; words are my armour and they are my weapons.' He took a deep breath and started to recite loudly and theatrically in French from a notebook he had pulled out of his trouser pocket. I thought I could make out something

which loosely translated as: 'My love is like a cat /
howling it howls / tearing my feelings apart / deep
within my bowels.'

Bernadette came dashing in at that point looking
flustered and begging him to stop, explaining that
our French simply wasn't good enough to appreciate
the nuances.

'Isn't that right?' she beseeched, looking at me with
imploring eyes.

'Absolutely true, my French is very basic,' I assured
him. 'I aspire to understand poetry, but I'm not there yet.'

Later, Bernadette told me that Thibault could
work himself into a melodramatic frenzy when
reciting poetry; first he would sigh, then cry tears of
unhappiness – which his many previous lovers had
apparently found intoxicatingly romantic. 'Extremely
exasperating if you are not romantically inclined
towards him, though,' she added.

'Why don't you stay for dinner?' asked Jean-Claude.
'Bernadette has prepared pigeon pie and Uncle
brought a wonderful chestnut cream cake which
Amandine made.'

'And you can have a taste of my rum – that'll put hairs
on your chest,' said Thibault, who had suddenly cheered
up, almost as if he'd been reset, and held his glass out for
a top-up of Armagnac and sparkling wine.

'Oh well, how can we resist that? A hairy-chested
woman does it for me,' said Mark.

Poetry wasn't mentioned again, but Thibault talked of his 'almost relationships' with some of the world's most beautiful women, including Catherine Deneuve, whom he claimed to have met in a record store in the Puces de Saint-Ouen flea market in Paris, and Jane Birkin, whom he said he had encountered at a bar on the Left Bank and consoled after she'd had a bust-up with Serge Gainsbourg.

Mark popped back to the house to feed and walk the dogs, make sure the cats were okay and stoke the wood fire so that we wouldn't freeze when we went home. We do sometimes wish that we'd installed central heating when we first came to France, but nothing beats a roaring log fire on a cold night.

While he was gone, Bernadette's friend Estelle dropped by with a goose for the Christmas Eve dinner. A no-nonsense farmer's wife in her forties, with a stout frame that was packed into a blue boiler suit, she seemed quite taken with Thibault's gallantry as he kissed her hand, which I thought was either brave of him or his rum had rendered him so senseless that he hadn't noticed her fingernails were caked with dried blood (no doubt from the poor goose rather than any foul play).

'Why don't you stay for dinner, m'dear?' said Thibault, giving her a gappy smile. He was certainly doing his best to make sure that, should Amandine leave him, he had a substitute lined up. Estelle declined, as she had 'a van-load of birds to deliver': 'I'm tempted all right, but that bugger of a husband of mine is nowhere to be seen and someone has to get this lot done.'

'My dear,' said Thibault, 'I would love you to visit me at my home in Ardèche one day.'

'Don't worry, you don't have to answer,' said Bernadette to Estelle. 'He asks everyone.'

When Mark returned, Thibault insisted that he try a drop of rum, which he assured him would warm his veins, even though our house was less than five minutes' walk away. He poured a small glass and handed it to Mark, who sniffed and visibly recoiled. He took the smallest of sips and breathed out deeply but didn't say a word; in fact, he hardly spoke for the rest of the night. Bernadette discreetly removed the glass when she served the pigeon pie, a dish which Mark later said he couldn't fully appreciate since the rum had actually numbed his mouth and rendered him speechless.

When we left to go home, Thibault gave us a bottle of rum as a parting gift. We took Bernadette's advice and later tipped it away in the garden over a particularly stubborn patch of weeds – it worked a treat.

The rest of December was very quiet, as it often is, but I have no problem with this. I am happy that the most talked-about event in the village is often something that Madame Bernadette has baked. Her Carambar tarte recipe, for instance, was discussed at length. Carambars are long and very chewy (pull-your-fillings-out-style) toffees. Legend has it that the French confectionery company that created them in 1954 did so by happy accident. Extra cocoa was mixed in with caramel to see what it tasted like, whereupon the machine developed a fault and spewed out long thin bars of sweet toffee – but everyone agreed they were delicious, so they kept the long-bar formula even though it's hard to get a whole one in your mouth! Carambars are very popular in France and apparently the company makes a whopping 82,000 kilometres of chewy toffee each year!

At some point, someone thought it would be a good idea to put jokes on the inside of the wrappers. They're pretty awful. For example: 'What is a female hamster?' Answer: 'Amsterdam.' Or: 'Why should you not tell jokes to a balloon?' Answer: 'It might burst out laughing.' Groan. Apparently, Carambar is responsible for one of the most popular jokes in France, which is not remotely funny to anyone but the French:

- *Maman, je peux avoir du chocolat?*
- *Il y en a dans le placard. Va donc te servir.*
- *Mais Maman, je peux pas. Tu sais bien que je n'ai pas de bras …*
- *Pas de bras, pas de chocolat!*

Translation:

- Mum, can I have some chocolate?
- There's some in the cupboard. Go get it.
- But Mum, I can't. You know very well that I don't have arms …
- No arms, no chocolate!

It isn't really a joke at all, it's just a selection of words that are absurd and rather sinister, but the expression '*pas de bras, pas de chocolat*' has passed into everyday language to indicate that something is impossible.

The most talked-about topic in our house was the local *pompiers* (firefighters) calendar. At the end of the year, the *pompiers*, most of them volunteers, visit all the villages that they support to give each resident a calendar, and we all offer a monetary gift in return as a thank-you for their hard work. There have been several times when I've been queuing up at the meat counter in our local supermarket and the butcher, a volunteer *pompier*, has received a text and had to leap away from the counter, rip off his apron and dash off to the fire station across the road, where he changes into his firefighting gear like a rather rotund Superman, jumps on the little red van with the rest of the team and speeds off to attend an incident.

That year's calendar featured a smouldering hay bale, a tractor churning out clouds of smoke and a wasps' nest. I'm not sure who chooses the photos, but they're certainly different from your usual type of firefighter calendar.

On Christmas Day, we went for a long walk with the dogs just as dusk fell. Unusually, shutters on many of the houses were open, and a warm glow fell from the windows, creating sparkles on the light dusting of snow that covered everything.

Wisps of smoke danced away from chimneys, disappearing over the tops of trees whose leafless branches were bowed with giant balls of mistletoe. A pure white stork stood alone in a field in the distance, until a deer ran out of the woods nearby and startled it into flying over a hill. A giant hare bounded across our path and the dogs were so surprised that they stood stock-still, leaving the hare to go safely on its way, not bothered by three ageing but still keen mutts. We trudged on, past empty fields and down silent roads. Owls hooted and a few hardy bats flew above our heads.

It was a silent night lit by a full moon, glowing through clouds. Claudette passed us on her way to Madame Bernadette's house. Wearing her winter coat and a thick woollen shawl over the top she stopped to say hello. 'Winter is on my head,' she said, smiling, 'but eternal spring is in my heart.'

CHAPTER 7

All you need is love. And cake …

'IT NEVER SNOWS in this village,' Jean-Claude had informed us with a straight face when we first met him. Our house then was just a place to camp in at the weekends and for holidays; most of the rooms were uninhabitable. One end of the property was held up by a metal pole and I will never forget my dad standing there, looking first at the pole, then at me, eyebrows raised, and telling me: 'This house is a money pit … you'll never be done.'

When the wind blew, the windows rattled in their frames; the metal farm doors that provided an entrance at the back of the house swung wildly back and forth, banging loudly enough to set off all the dogs in the village. The roof was like a sieve through which the frequent rain fell.

An open pipe ran from the garden into what we

laughingly called the 'utility room' on the ground floor, on account of the broken washing machine left behind by the previous owner. Small and very much unwanted creatures entered the house via the pipe. We placed a net over the end of it, only to find it chewed and discarded. We put a metal colander over the opening and tied it tight, but the creatures heaved it off. We bunged the pipe up with old socks and rags, but the wily trespassers were undaunted and simply pilfered the stuffing to use it to line their nests with. Rats and mice made the house their own when we weren't around to scare them off. We never did work out what the pipe was meant for, and eventually removed it and sealed off the entrance. But the rats and mice adapted, and began to make their way in through other holes. And when it snowed, the *fouines* arrived.

We are from London, where it snows rarely and moderately. We figured that Jean-Claude was joking when he said it didn't snow, but since we are only 150 miles from London as the crow flies, albeit in a different country, we expected it would be a similar sort of snowfall.

We were wrong.

In our first year of living in France, it snowed so heavily that it reached the ground-floor windowsills. Thierry the farmer dashed into action with his tractor, clearing the roads so that he could get to his fields and barns. But in doing so, he blocked us in with piles of snow of up to 2.5 metres deep, which hardened overnight to form an icy wall so that we had to dig our way out. During periods of bad weather, accessible houses become a very attractive proposition to all sorts of animals. When we first cleared out the loft, alongside the rats and mice and empty wasps' nests, we discovered what we thought were skeletons of small cats. They were strewn over the thick layer of dried earth embedded with animal hair and twigs, which had been applied by previous occupants as a primitive form of insulation. I can't tell you how much fun it wasn't to remove it all by hand. It was filthy work and took weeks to do as it was smeared up the walls and over the floors, and had been there for many, many years.

It turned out that the skeletons weren't cats but in fact *fouines*, known in English as stone martens or beech martens – small creatures related to weasels and stoats.

Over the next few years, we fixed the holes in the roof. We insulated and plastered and made the house watertight and by invitation only. Several winters of light snowfall followed. But then came a winter which brought with it a blizzard of the white stuff, blanketing the village and the countryside for miles around. Children dragged out old toboggans and whizzed down the frozen hills, and built scarf-wearing snowmen on the village green. Bread Man, Fish Man and Groceries Man did a roaring trade as no one wanted to slide up and down the steep roads of the valleys to go to the shops. There were queues when their vans arrived, and we and our neighbours, bundled up against the cold, slid along slippery streets and chatted as we waited to shop, comparing this year's snow to that of ten years ago, or even fifty years ago for some residents. We fed logs into the fire all day long to keep warm and regularly checked on elderly neighbours.

We didn't worry about the creatures in the loft, though, as we thought we'd thwarted them. But *fouines* are clever animals and wily: they can squeeze into the smallest openings and so, unimpressed with the harsh weather, they returned, making their way back to the place they had once called home. They are the very worst type of house guest, being both noisy and smelly. There is little height in the loft – Mark can just about crawl around up there if needs be, but with all the insulation it's not a good place to be. We banged on the ceiling at night when they started their scratching and squeaking. The noise would stop for several minutes, then start again.

'Play music all night long,' suggested Jean-Claude. 'They can't stand it and they'll soon be off.'

The first night we tried it, the creatures were inactive. We were gleeful. They must hate the music, we said to each other, they're packing their bags, moving out. But the next evening they were active again, and the night after that.

'*Bah*,' said Jean-Claude dismissively. 'What are you playing? Disco music from the eighties? *Non, non, non,* they are dancing up there. Try something heavier with a lot of banging drums, a bit of that should be enough to get rid of them ...'

We were dubious, but desperate for the dancing martens to depart. We played AC/DC, Black Sabbath and Motörhead. Well, apparently *fouines* like heavy metal music too. The sound of their claws scratching above our heads drove us to distraction, and 'Ace of Spades' was stuck in my mind for an entire day.

'Try petrol,' advised Thierry. 'They can't stand the smell. Stick a bowl of it up there.'

We were dubious about this, and it also sounded dangerous. But we had to do something. We put a small bowl of petrol inside a big bowl and hoped that the *fouines* wouldn't knock it over while the stink did its thing to make them depart at full speed.

But not these *fouines* – they couldn't care less. They seemed to love the odour of petrol. To them it was like Chanel No. 5.

'I could shoot them for you if you like,' said Petit Frère. 'I can go up there after supper. I'll lie in wait in the corner, you won't even know I'm there. Then when they come in: bang, bang, bang. Problem solved.'

We thanked him for his kind offer, but decided that the idea of him sitting above our heads with his shotgun, firing bullets into the floor from a confined crouching position as he tracked the offending creatures throughout the night, was probably not a good one.

'Get the pest man in,' declared Madame Bernadette, running a finger from left to right across her throat.

We didn't want to go down that route if we could help it, as we were worried about the cats, but to tell the truth it was rapidly getting to the 'it's the *fouines* or me' stage.

'We'll think about it,' I said, knowing there was nothing to think about. We all have to live the best we can in our environment and clearly the *fouines* had come to the logical conclusion that prior to our arrival the empty house was up for grabs, and so as they were there first, or at least before us, they felt entitled to stay there. But their wee was starting to stain the ceiling and we had developed huge bags under our eyes after being woken up so often throughout the night.

It was Monsieur and Madame Pepperpot who came to the rescue in the end. The topic of the soft-hearted *Anglais* who refused to do the deed with the filthy *fouines* had been widely discussed in the village to the point where even the diminutive couple, who rarely socialize other than with their beloved cows, had heard of our issues.

'Mothballs,' said Madame Pepperpot. She'd popped to the town hall at the bottom of our little road to get some papers photocopied and dropped by to offer us her thoughts.

'Chuck a handful of the strongest mothballs you can find up into the loft, and those pesky animals will be gone by morning.'

She was absolutely right.

The night after we had followed her advice, we slept undisturbed until late in the morning when we heard 'beep, beep, beep'. It was the sound of a horn echoing around the Seven Valleys and bouncing off the snow-covered hills, making any dogs unlucky enough to be outside on the cold day bark a warning. It was Bread Man.

We hurriedly dressed to go to meet him and pick up our Saturday treat from the side window of his van where he displays his cakes of the day. It's a French habit that we've happily adopted. On the whole, the French are not big snackers, but a weekly treat is a must. There's a chocolate shop called Au Chat Bleu in the nearby town of Le Touquet, which was opened in 1912 by two sisters who loved cats, particularly Persian Blues. Go there on a Saturday and you will find many old folk among the customers, and if you ask them nicely, they will tell you how long they have been visiting Au Chat Bleu to buy their Saturday treat. For some of them it's been more than seventy years, ever loyal to the magical chocolate shop that makes you feel as though you've stepped back in time.

Bread Man is also a fan of chocolate and his *trois chocolats* cakes are irresistible; the layers of crispy biscuit and chocolate vied for attention with Viennese pastries in the mouth-watering presentation.

'Can I take a photo?' I asked him.

'As you wish,' he said, raising bushy black eyebrows under his blue workman's cap.

'Why do you want photos of my buns?' he enquired, as I held my phone over a tray of beautiful golden brioche buns flavoured with chocolate, raisins and vanilla sugar.

'They are beautiful,' I said, 'like little works of art.' That clearly pleased him – his moustache quivered above a big smile. 'Plus, I have a lot of friends all around the world who love to see cake photos on Facebook.'

'Not the same as tasting them,' he remarked, smiling when I showed him the photo, 'but we can dream, we can imagine, shut our eyes and smell the sweet buttery scent of a golden flaky croissant just out of the oven, of sweet salty caramel oozing from a profiterole, of chocolate squeezing out of a delicious éclair or a decadent Chantilly-cream-smothered Saint Honoré cake with fresh, fragrant strawberries … Imagination gives wings to your dreams.'

A philosophical baker is not anywhere as unusual as you might imagine. France has a love affair with philosophy that goes way back. The French Revolution was influenced by one of France's favourite philosophers, Denis Diderot, a writer who was one of the leading minds of the so-called Age of Enlightenment period in France. Long before the French Revolution, he prophetically wrote: 'Man will never be free until the last king is strangled with the entrails of the last priest.' You'll find streets and squares dedicated to him all over

France. It's rumoured that you'll even have to answer questions on Diderot and philosophy if you take the French citizenship test.

More recently, the philosopher and writer Jean-Paul Sartre was the darling of the French. He featured on a TV news bulletin in 1951, which apparently went down so well with viewing audiences that by the year 2000 there had been more than 3,500 programmes on French TV about philosophy. Bookshops are stacked with huge tomes on the topic, and it's also possible for philosophers to attain celebrity status in France and appear on the covers of magazines. The study of philosophy is mandated on the French school curriculum. And when those kids grow up, they still love to talk philosophy. There are even philosophical events and festivals. Emmanuel Macron, President of France, was a student of philosophy, and French newspapers love to surmise how his studies have a bearing on his policies.

If you ever go to dinner with a French person, be prepared to tackle philosophy in some form or other. The first time it happened to me was in the lovely Loir region (yes Loir, no 'e'; it neighbours the Loire with the 'e'). We were staying at a *chambre d'hôte*, a B&B owned by the village mayor who lived in a mini château next door. He invited us to dine with him one night, and over the meal the whole family, including teenage kids, discussed the works of the great French writer Alexandre Dumas, and in particular his outlook that: 'Learning does not make one learned: there are those who have knowledge and those who have understanding. The first requires memory and the second philosophy.'

Bread Man's philosophy was that you should have your cake and eat it too. Of course, I couldn't resist buying two of the little brioche buns.

'See you soon,' he said, and drove off to Madame Bernadette, who was waiting impatiently for her bread at the gate of her little cottage at the bottom of the hill.

I've not got round to telling him that my neighbour Constance has taught me how to make pretty good brioche. My first few years in France were a culinary disaster as far as my neighbours were concerned, and although several neighbours tried to teach me, they soon came to realize that while I was pretty good at eating food, I was useless at preparing it. I was a somewhat lazy cook, and I'm still happy to leave Mark to deal with things in the kitchen but, after several years of travelling around France, indulging in diverse regional cuisines, meeting amazing chefs and having lessons with professionals, I'm far less 'flop chef', as my friends nicknamed me.

Constance and her husband Guillaume live in Lille, but they spend every weekend and holiday at their fortified stone-built farmhouse in our village. Her kitchen looks as if it has been transported from a medieval castle. The stone walls are painted a milky white, while the oak beams are blackened and split with age. A large wooden table, on which there is always a jug of flowers and often a basket of vegetables or fruit from the garden, dominates the room, and there are a few wobbly old chairs.

Along one wall is a fireplace that's large enough to fit a chair inside, but instead contains copper pans dangling from hooks. There's a sizeable stove, a stone sink and several wooden cupboards full of plates, tablecloths, jugs, jars, cups, bowls and cutlery, while shelf after shelf feature an abundance of tins, packets, bottles and containers. Pans and cauldrons are suspended from the ceiling, and sometimes onions, garlic or great bunches of hops hang drying, filling the house with the scent of the countryside.

Constance is a brilliant cook; her tarts are frequent winners in local baking contests and when it came to my lack of skill in the kitchen, she was determined not to give up on me. She has coached and coaxed me along, inviting me to her home to watch her cook, progressing to being allowed to help measure ingredients, mix, stir, chop and eventually to taste the food as it's being prepared, and try to understand the flavours, the seasonings, the spices. I will never be at the same level as her, but I can now make a passable brioche in an emergency.

I can even make bread, though I don't tend to bother because I know that however much I practise, I will never be as good as Bread Man. French bread-makers are a different breed from your average bread-maker. Take Alex Croquet, a baker from the north with two boulangeries in Lille, including a very famous store in rue Esquermoise where you'll also find Méert, a sweet shop and patisserie established over 170 years ago that's beautifully furnished with ancient cabinets. Alex takes bread-making to a whole new level. It's rumoured that he even takes his sourdough starter on holiday with him so he can keep feeding it. In the Seven Valleys, it's said that the Goat Lady, who makes goats' cheese and bakes bread in a huge stone bread oven, uses a sourdough starter that is more than 200 years old, fed and nurtured through generations of her family. And even for amateur bakers, bread is a serious hobby.

My first bread-making lesson was several years ago. I was visiting my English friends Gary and Annette, who live in a tiny hamlet close by, where, just as in my village, everyone knows everyone and there are no shops or bars. It's a place that seems pickled in the past. On the corner of the narrow track that leads to their house is an ancient church, and on the wall there are a few words engraved in Latin: '*Do not take our bells for cannon*' – a message from the locals of the sixteenth century to any potential marauding armies in the area, after the Army of Flanders, a multinational army in the service of the King of Spain, passed this way and stole the church's large bronze bells.

Annette, a retired nurse, and her husband Gary, an orator of history, thought that they were the only residents on the tiny lane leading off the town's main road, which meanders up into the tree-covered hills where the fields of sheep and cows drink from the skinny Créquoise stream that wriggles to meet the Canche River and flows on to the English Channel. But on my way to visit them, I noticed that the rather ramshackle house at the bottom of their little lane had wisps of smoke coming from the chimney. I mentioned it to Annette and she decided that we should go and investigate.

We pushed our way past bushes that hung over the cobbled path, climbed a moss-covered step and rapped on the wooden door. The top half of the door swung inwards and a man leaned out. He was middle-aged with dark curly hair and a bushy moustache, and he peered at us through thick glasses.

'*Bonjour,* I'm your neighbour Annette and this is my friend Janine. We thought we'd come and say hello.'

'*Bonjour mesdames,*' replied the man. 'I am making bread, please do come in.'

We stepped into a gloomy room. The only light came from a couple of hurricane lamps hanging from the beamed ceiling, casting a soft glow over a long, low wooden table strewn with china bowls and stone bottles. Two cats lazed on the cream-coloured tiled floor in front of a roaring wood fire; they narrowed their eyes at us but didn't move.

'*Oh là là, jolie, jolie,*' a high-pitched voice screeched, and as my eyes became accustomed to the dull light, I caught a flash of bright green in the dimness. I had to look twice to make sure I hadn't gone bonkers. A parakeet was balanced on the edge of a cooking pot that had been placed on top of the stove.

'Gaston,' said the man, 'say hello to our neighbours.'

'*Allo, allo, oh là là, jolie, jolie,*' squawked the bird, its head bobbing up and down in unison with its feet as it hopped round its culinary perch.

Beckoning us to sit at stools at the table, the man poured coffee into two bowls and introduced himself. His name was Gaspard and he lived most of the year in his castle in the Ardennes, in the north-east of France – just a small castle, nothing out of the ordinary, he insisted. He had inherited this rather derelict old house from an uncle many years ago and he visited just a few times each year for a short while. I could understand why after he informed us that the property had no electricity and no running water, but, he said, it didn't matter, as there were two wells in the garden which were good in an emergency. I've looked down a few wells in France, and there are often dead birds and toads and more vile things floating in the water. He must have seen me shudder as he assured us the coffee had been made with bottled water. The walls of the room were covered in faded wallpaper, red flowers with small green leaves on a washed-out yellow background. Tattered, spleen-coloured velvet curtains hung at windows whose shutters were firmly closed and a pair of armchairs with embroidered covers were set before the fire. There were piles of books everywhere. The warmth from the wood fire and the smell of the bread cooking in the oven were timeless and comforting, and I wondered for a moment if by crossing the threshold we had stepped back into the nineteenth century.

Gaspard spoke very good English. He was a former wine export manager for a well-known champagne house and a food critic for several newspapers, and he had spent time in America in the 1970s working on a vineyard. He had also been employed by a wine company in England, where he had developed a taste for piccalilli (a mustardy pickle), which he said is the perfect accompaniment to steaming French *boudin noir* (blood sausages). We stayed for an hour watching him make bread, rolling, kneading and shaping the dough, and he told us of his uncle who had owned the house and who had in turn inherited it from a distant aunt.

'My uncle was an artist and would come here to capture the beautiful countryside on canvas, accompanied by his pet monkey – he was rather eccentric.' He said this without a trace of irony as the parakeet flew around the room screeching '*oh là là*' and then picked its way daintily across the table where the dough was being worked.

'Ah, you want attention, my little Gaston,' he said, picking the bird up and gently kissing it on the beak. 'Oh, you want to go out?'

Gaspard opened the front door and the bird flew off. Five minutes later, he opened the door and called, 'Gaston, come in now,' and the parakeet flew straight back in. I have to admit to a little jealousy; I rarely get any of my animals to do anything I tell them, unless a bribe is involved, and even then I'm never sure whether I will be successful or not. Later, Annette told me about another time that Gaspard had come to stay at the cottage, when, despite his cats being as well behaved and obedient as Gaston, one of them had wandered off at an inopportune moment. Gaspard delayed his departure for as long as he could, but he eventually had to leave without his pet and was distraught. The cat, of course, since they are almost all contrary creatures, returned an hour after he'd gone, and Annette ended up looking after it for six weeks until Gaspard's next visit.

Annette and Gary became good friends with their neighbour over time. Eventually, he tired of living without electricity and had a cable laid to the house. He asked Gary, a former electrician, to help him sort out a TV he had bought but couldn't get to work properly. Gary was more than happy to help and immediately spotted the problem when he saw a satellite dish swinging in the wind as it hung from a tree in Gaspard's garden. He explained that the dish needed to be fixed to the wall of the house, but the branches of a nearby tree were in the way. No problem, Gaspard had said, inviting Gary into the house where he was horrified to find that from a single plug socket there were several extension leads hosting plugs for lamps, a computer, electric heaters and a fridge. As Gary stood stressing about the fire hazard, he heard loud bangs from the garden and discovered that Gaspard, having first wielded a chainsaw to cut off the lower branches of the tree, was now attempting to shoot the higher branches off with a shotgun. Gaspard is the sort of man who tackles everything head on with whatever tools are to hand.

Sometimes Gary and Annette would hear him cursing in the garden late at night and would watch from the window as he stumbled around, a torch strapped to his head, trying to avoid falling into the wells. Apparently, he always 'checked out strange noises' as he once later told them when they asked.

One chilly day we were at Gary and Annette's house where Mark was helping Gary to mend a fence in the back of the garden. If you think I'm bad with my animal family of more than sixty animals, then you'll be impressed by Annette's fifteen cats, two dogs, two goats, two turkeys, fifty ducks and more than a hundred chickens of several types. The devilish goats Heidi and Hannah had kicked the fence down, and the birds were wandering about all over the lane, dashing out of the way of passing tractors and roosting on the church wall.

Annette and I were sitting chatting when Gaspard arrived and asked if Gary would help him to reverse his trailer through the gates to his garden. Mark came in for tea while Gary went off with Gaspard. Even indoors we could hear a car being furiously revved, the squealing of brakes, more loud revving and Gary shouting. We wandered out to the front of the house and watched as Gary misdirected Gaspard in his 4x4, on the back of which was an empty trailer measuring about 1.5 metres wide and 1.5 metres long.

'*Droite*, left, I mean *gauche* ... stop ... right, *droite*, stop.' Gary's instructions confused and exasperated Gaspard.

'*Merde, putain*,' said Gaspard, cursing as his wheels slid about in the narrow mossy entrance to his garden and the trailer locked first to the left, then to the right. He drove the car back and forth, becoming more and more frustrated, but still unable to manoeuvre the trailer through the gates.

'Can I help?' asked Mark.

'*Oui, oui*,' replied Gaspard, getting out of the car. 'Take the keys, you drive.'

But instead, Mark walked to the back of the car, unhooked the trailer – which wasn't remotely heavy – and simply pushed it through manually.

Gary swore under his breath, while Annette and I burst out laughing.

Gaspard stood open-mouthed before muttering: 'Twenty years I've had a problem getting that *merde* of a trailer through those gates, twenty years.'

CHAPTER 8

The feast of the gods

'COME TO OURS next Saturday for dinner at seven o'clock, and don't be late! I've read your books, I know you think you should arrive "à la French time", but on this occasion, I mean it,' said Valérie, our Parisian neighbour (known to her friends as Vava), without drawing breath. 'Oui? It's okay?'

We were at the Friday-morning market on an early, not-very-summery day in the town of Étaples-sur-Mer.

'*Bon*. See you Saturday,' she said after I'd agreed. And after two cheek kisses, off she went, dashing through the crowds in typically hasty Parisian fashion, her blonde hair immaculately coiffed as always, smartly turned out in her tailored jeans and trench coat, her heels clicking on the cobbles.

I was at the back of a line of customers all waiting patiently as the lady at the front peered at several boxes containing a variety of apples, frowning and chewing her lip as she tried to make up her mind which ones to buy. I caught the drift of her conversation with the vendor: 'My husband likes them sweet, my daughter likes them sharp.'

No one in the queue huffed and puffed, no one tapped their feet impatiently. Picking the right food takes time; it's something to be appreciated. When I first lived in France, I didn't get it at all. We would be astounded in local supermarkets that till servers would stop work to chat to customers, asking about their health, their families, exchanging kisses across the counter. There is rarely a rush to swish items across the scanner and I suspect that if speedy beeps were ever heard, a manager would appear, fearing a technical issue. I've learned that it's not about the wait, it's about the attitude. You can get away with a lot in France – disagree with someone, speak poor French, dislike cheese – but there's no excuse for a bad attitude. Eventually, the lady chose three different types of apple and we all shuffled forward.

I finished my shopping and was rewarded with a gift of two pears from the jovial vendor. He was well wrapped up against the wintry drizzle that was falling from a turtle-dove-grey sky and wearing a bright-yellow fisherman's sou'wester, perfectly dressed for both the weather and fishing-village location.

Étaples, or 'Eat Apples' as it was nicknamed by British Tommies stationed here in the First World War, is not actually 'sur-mer' but on the estuary of the River Canche, which flows from the hardly-heard-of but pretty village of Gouy-en-Ternois in Pas-de-Calais, through Picardy and back into Pas-de-Calais where it meets the English Channel at Le Touquet on the Opal Coast. It's a lively little fishing port, joined to Le Touquet via a pink granite bridge. Many people drive straight through Étaples, but it's one of those places that has plenty of charm if you know where to look.

It was once an important town: it's claimed that King Henry VIII of England once stayed here in the now long-gone castle.

And if you think glamping is a modern invention – think again. A little over a mile from the town of Guînes, on an area of neutral ground, Henry VIII and Francis I of France convened for their famous meeting in June 1520, ostensibly to put their differences aside in a quest for peace. For eighteen days, each monarch did his best to outshine the other by setting up equally ostentatious camps in Ardres (François) and Guînes (Henry). François hung his tents with cloths made from real gold thread that gleamed in the June sun. He draped his horses with gold cloth too, and some of them even wore gold shoes. Not to be outdone, as well as erecting hundreds of tents and a tiltyard for jousting, Henry also had a massive temporary palace built. It took many hundreds of workmen to erect it. Covered with canvas sheets painted to look like stone, it even had stained-glass windows and fountains at the entrance from which poured forth wine for Henry's guests – an estimated 5,000 of them – all decked out in their finest clothes and jewels, and including, it's thought, a young lady-in-waiting to François' wife Queen Claude, named Anne Boleyn. The kings jousted, partied like there was no tomorrow and spent money like it was water. The meeting ended with a Catholic Mass and a declaration of friendship and peace. A year later, the glory days of summer fun were forgotten and they were back to their old, warmongering ways.

Almost 300 years later, Napoléon Bonaparte stayed in Étaples, toying with the idea of invading England. Nowadays it's a peaceful little place, and the Place du Général de Gaulle, where the market is held, is lined with shops, restaurants and bars. Mark and I love to go to BiBoViNo for an aperitif, before enjoying the best fish and chips in France at SoFish round the corner in the Boulevard de l'Impératrice.

Étaples market is one of the biggest in the Pas-de-Calais department and the town has the additional allure of several *poissonneries*, which sell fish freshly caught off the Opal Coast, luring customers from far and wide. The stalls spread from the front of the town hall in the Place du Général de Gaulle, then wind along side streets, past the patisseries, fromageries, clothes shops, the cosy Café de l'Hotel de Ville and the brasserie Au Vieux Port, where they serve great steaming pots of fresh mussels and crisp *frites*, the taste of northern France.

This bustling market is known as the 'housewives'

favourite', though in fact it's even been voted the favourite market of the entire French population. And yes, they do have a favourite market contest in France. And a favourite village. Favourite farm too. Most beautiful detour. Favourite monument. Most charming chicken and most handsome cockerel. It's a French thing to be competitive. Vava once told me that there's a belief in France that being competitive means constantly improving, and that by judging others you can help them to up their game. But it's also about recognition and a lot about marketing, something at which the French are experts.

Napoléon may have criticized the British for being a 'nation of shopkeepers', but in fact it was the French who invented the concept of the department store with Le Bon Marché in Paris, which also introduced free shipping on most purchases over 25 francs in 1852. The French were also the first to transmit online news – and it wasn't via the internet but through Minitel, a small-screen terminal connected to the telephone line which made a hissing noise. Work began on its design in France in 1978 and trials got underway in 1980. In the 1990s, there were 9 million sets in use at one point. Users in France could view the news, search phone directories, check their horoscopes and bank accounts, buy train tickets and chat online. At its peak there were some 25,000 services available through Minitel. One of the other significant things that Minitel offered was online sex chats. Known by those in the know as 'Minitel Rose', the world's first electronic cybersex was initiated on this clunky old service and it spawned a multimillion franc/euro industry. But Minitel never took off anywhere outside France. Incredibly, there were some 400,000 users still accessing services until, with no hope of ever truly competing with the internet, the plug was officially pulled on 30 June 2012.

Markets are like a tiny snapshot of France whether you're in the north, south, east or west, and very little changes from one decade, or even one century, to the next. There will always be clusters of people chatting – the market is one of the most, if not *the* most, social event of the week. Old men will be sat at tables outside the *tabac* on warm days and inside on cold days, sipping tiny cups of coffee or a stirring nip of Calvados to celebrate having escaped from following their basket-carrying, trolley-pulling wives from stall to stall. Savvy boulangeries will open their doors so that the waft of just-baked bread and pastries lures punters in, unable to resist the enticing aroma of baguettes and croissants. Church bells will ring on the hour and everyone will stop to look at their watch when they hear it to confirm the time, especially if there are eleven chimes, keen to finish up before the sacred two hours set aside for lunch. Old ladies will congregate at the *pharmacie* to discuss their ailments and pills, their knee and hip replacements. If you're considered a good customer –

that is, if you go often enough to the same stall or spend a decent amount of money there – you'll be rewarded with a gift of seasonal fruit or a couple of sausages from the butcher, guaranteed to make you feel like an insider. If you ever want to feel the soul of a village, go to its market.

The great American cook Julia Child once said: 'In France, cooking is a serious art form and a national sport.' And when you go to a French market, even a teeny, tiny one like my local market in Beaurainville, you know this is true. People appreciate each thing, whether it's a cabbage or a wedge of Camembert. They chat to the seller about its qualities, discuss how to cook or serve it. The markets are still the heart of France.

Beaurainville market has everything you need to cook a great meal despite its diminutive size. It has a fabulous fish stall run by two ladies who also sell wonderful sauces. A butcher-delicatessen van is there, manned by members of the Dhalleine family who, for four generations, have run their renowned butcher shop in the nearby village of Loison-sur-Créquoise. And there's a dairy stall selling local and national cheeses as well as handmade butter. On other stands you can buy salad in season and outstanding home-grown vegetables – potatoes and carrots with the mud still on them – and there are bags of mixed veg and local legumes sold with a bunch of herbs to make a robust stew. Some weeks there are a couple of clothes stalls and they are not exactly à la mode, but this is where we all go to support our regional producers and sellers and to catch up on the news.

The following Saturday, in faithful observance of Vava's instructions, Mark and I arrived at the home of the Parisians just as the village church bells struck seven o'clock. We'd walked the short distance from our house halfway up a hill, past the town hall, down a narrow stony pathway which eventually – if you follow it all the way along, passing fields of wheat, maize and sometimes peas, and on to the ancient church with its stained-glass windows – reaches a petite hamlet of just fifteen inhabitants. Small villages are strung like pearls throughout this region, joined by a network of ancient roads that meander through forests and fields, over hills and across streams, an alternative to the modern tarmac roads and still very much used.

'What's so important about being here at seven o'clock?' I asked as we were welcomed indoors.

'I wanted to see if you would,' laughed Vava. 'I told my other guests, who are all French, to be here at the same time to see what would happen – you are so *Duntun* Abbey!'

Vava is a fan of what she calls 'British manners' and, like, many of our French friends, she loves the *Downton Abbey* TV series. She was clearly delighted that we were the first to arrive and so punctual, thereby proving a point that the British are weird about being on time, unlike the French.

The next guest arrived fifteen minutes after us, which for the French is perfectly punctual. It's called the *le quart d'heure de politesse* or *le quart d'heure de courtoisie* or even *le quart d'heure Parisien* or *Toulousain* depending on where you live. It's accepted that guests will be anything from five to thirty minutes late when asked to dinner in France. I guess you could call it the *quart d'heure des Sept Vallées* around here.

Vava introduced us to Pascale, and we realized that we'd already met him once before a couple of years previously. It was at a Bastille Day party at a town hall in a village several miles away – an event we were unlikely to forget. We'd been invited by our Dutch friends Anika and Bas who had a second home there. Pascale, a short, stocky man with a full head of chestnut-coloured hair and an easy smile, was collecting ticket money at the entrance to a big marquee set up in the town hall car park.

'Aha, you're on the cosmopolitan table,' he said as we paid for our tickets and mentioned our Dutch friends. '*Bon courage!*'

'Strange,' said Mark. 'Why would we need good luck?'

We found Anika and Bas and discovered that they had gathered together a group of non-French friends to share a table: two couples from Belgium plus a British couple who were in their late sixties. We all introduced ourselves and the Brits wanted to know what everyone did for a living – mainly, it seemed, so that they could then tell us all how important they had been in their respective jobs. Mr S. was a former CEO of a multinational company in charge of hundreds of people, and Mrs S. had been a telecommunications director and had travelled the world.

Normally, just wine and beer would be served at this sort of event, but on this occasion there were also Martinis on offer and the British couple quaffed them with enthusiasm. Two hours later, with Martini supplies long gone, bottles of wine had made their way to the table, which Mr and Mrs S. knocked back as if it were going out of fashion. It was a hot night, the music was loud and the wine kept flowing. Festive meals are slow to start and even slower to finish, but thanks to the efforts of two little girls, who were helping their parents in the kitchen, plates of small spicy sausages were carefully delivered to each of the tables, and then they dashed back to the kitchen to collect more.

'Where,' demanded Mrs S. of Pascale, who had moved from the ticket desk to bar services and was delivering yet more wine to our table, 'is the main meal?'

'Madame, I shall make sure you get your food before anyone else,' he replied.

A chubby, chocolate-coloured Labrador that had been wandering from table to table seeking attention lay across my feet and I stared down at it with intense concentration, not wanting to look at anyone else on the table and wishing I was somewhere else.

'I want to dance,' said the inebriated woman, flinging her arms up into the air as the DJ played a medley of Beatles songs.

'Oh God,' muttered Anika, loud enough for us all to hear, 'please don't.'

Thankfully, Pascale arrived at our table bearing a tray full of plates of vegetable salad drizzled with a lively citrus dressing. It never ceases to amaze me how a group of volunteers in a makeshift kitchen can turn out dishes that taste as though they were created by professional chefs.

'*Voilà, madame*,' he said, placing a plate in front of the British woman, before turning to the rest of us. Everyone thanked him profusely, as though he'd told us that he'd turned water into wine. The people on the other tables were all looking at us.

Several couples got up to dance, unable to resist the sound of 'Twist and Shout'. They were joined by the two young girls who, freed from their sausage-delivery duties, were spinning around the jiving adults. The rotund Labrador left its bed on my feet and wandered in among them, wagging its tail and getting in the way of the enthusiastic revellers until Pascale coaxed it to go outside, where it flopped down and watched the smokers gathering together to blow fumes into the night sky.

Mrs S. never got to join in the dancing. By the time The Beatles had finished belting out their demand to 'shake it, shake it, shake it, baby, now', she had fallen asleep face down in her salad.

'It's her medication,' said her husband, patting her hand vigorously and yelling in her ear to wake her. He pulled her out of the chair and attempted to wipe the salad dressing from her face as she blinked at us. 'She gets tired, so I think I'll take her home.'

Afterwards, we'd chatted to Pascale who assured us there was nothing to be embarrassed about regarding our compatriots' conduct, as the couple had lived in the village for more than twenty years and behaved the same way at every event.

'It's okay,' he said kindly. 'It teaches the children that drinking too much is not a good thing.'

Pascale had come alone to dinner at the Parisians' as his partner, a policeman and a friend of Vava and her husband Hubert, had had to work.

Next to arrive was Jacqueline, Vava's mother. She was svelte with an immaculate short blonde bob, just like her daughter. She wore an elegant black trouser suit, accessorized with an eye-catching necklace, several friendship bracelets, white sneakers and a tiny handbag – an instant giveaway that she wasn't a local – here, big bags and wicker baskets, perfect for holding something foraged or swapped, are de rigueur. Entering the room amid a waft of expensive perfume, she told us she had just driven from Paris after having lunch with a handsome young man whom she'd met in a bookshop a few days before, remarking, 'A woman cannot live by bread, books and wine alone.' Vava rolled her eyes and shook her head at her mother.

'I bought it with my new eyes,' she said when I admired her necklace. 'In the past few months, my eyesight deteriorated to the point that unless I was about two to three metres away, I couldn't see details, no facial features. I couldn't read sizes or prices, so I bought items blindly. And on cloudy days it was even worse; I couldn't see the cyclists or the annoying e-scooters until they were almost on top of me. Reading was impossible – I even tried using two pairs of glasses, one on top of the other.'

'Yes, it's true, very embarrassing,' said Vava. 'She did it in restaurants to read the menu.'

'So,' continued Jacqueline, 'I had the laser surgery on both eyes and as soon as the laser intervention was finished, a burst of light appeared. Objects had dimensions, instead of a dull flat surface. I could look inside the open windows of the apartments opposite and see people's faces. I could read all the notices on the walls and on products. Colours and dimensions were very defined. It felt as if, after decades of living in a Magrittean greyness, I was stepping into a Van Gogh painting. As I walked along the rue Saint-Honoré, I was amazed at the depth of colour, the details of the architecture. I read every licence plate and every sign for advertising that I came upon. I wanted to dance on the pavement. Paris appeared like a landscape after a spring storm: clear, joyful and new.

'I went into a dress shop and checked my eyes in a mirror to see if they were bloodshot, and an old woman stared back at me. It was *moi*. I thought I might have to tell the ophthalmologist I wanted my money back, for I had aged by ten years during the procedure. Now I can see every wrinkle on my face. It is like a rebirth, like a newborn baby that's all wrinkly, but still, I am happy.'

We applauded her. How could you not?

'Oh please don't encourage her,' said Vava. 'She talks way too much.'

The last two guests to arrive were former Parisians Mimi and Georges, a middle-aged couple who had settled in the north to manage a *gîte* instead of moving to the south as Parisians are supposed to do.

'I am thinking of retiring from teaching,' Vava said, 'and *maman* and I are thinking of opening a little bistro in Paris. So tonight, we will cook dishes that we would propose to put on our menu, and we want you to be honest and tell us what you think. We will serve you plates to share so you can try a little of everything.'

Vava headed to the tiny cottage kitchen with Jacqueline. The guests were sat on high stools around a wooden table, and Hubert poured more wine and told us stories about his life as a *flic* in Paris, and how once there was a man who robbed bakeries wielding a baguette as if it were a gun and demanding cakes before running out with them.

Jacqueline returned with tiny bowls of pea soup in which floated slivers of smoked ham and purple edible flowers. There was a plateful of miniature toasted *croque monsieur* with ham and Comté cheese from the Jura mountains and a bowl of perfectly poached eggs served with early asparagus spears and a silky-smooth hollandaise sauce.

Then it was steak and *frites*. When I was young, the pinnacle of sophistication was going to a steakhouse for steak and chips, usually served with peas, fried tomatoes, mushrooms and onions. The meat would be tough and, according to my dad, 'properly cooked', which meant it had the consistency of boot leather.

In France, cooking steak this way and covering the taste with multiple other foodstuffs is an insult. We once took my dad for steak and *frites* at a bistro in the shadow of the UNESCO-listed, fourteenth-century belfry of Béthune in the town's Grand'Place, which is famous for its carillon of thirty-seven bells that ring out chirpy tunes every quarter of an hour. The waiter came to our table to take our orders and we had what you might call 'a situation'. We later referred to it as 'Steakgate'.

'How would you like your steak cooked?' asked the waiter.

Mark and I requested medium to well done, knowing full well that what we would get would be medium rare.

'Well done, very well done,' said Dad.

'I'm sorry, Sir, Chef doesn't do very well done. The steak is simply too good. It would be a crime to scorch it.'

'But I want it well done.'

'Then you will have to go elsewhere. Or have something else.' The waiter walked off to the kitchen muttering under his breath as Dad sat there absolutely flabbergasted.

'I'm the customer, why can't I have my steak well done?'

Then, the chef emerged from the kitchen in his white apron with the waiter who pointed to our table.

'*Monsieur,*' the chef said to Dad, 'I hear that you wish for your steak to be very well done? But you see, it would be a sin, it would ruin my reputation if my customers were to witness a steak being delivered as you wish. But I will cook you a steak as well done as I possibly can, and if you do not enjoy it, you will not have to pay. Are we agreed?'

We were. 'Free steak for me then,' said Dad, behind the retreating chef's back, and we promised to take him for a burger afterwards if necessary.

It's not that unusual that the customer isn't always king in France. I once went into a clothes shop in

Montreuil-sur-Mer having fallen in love with a dress I'd seen in the window. 'Do you have it in my size?' I asked the very chic, stick-thin woman behind the counter. She looked me up and down as if I was a talking turd. '*Non*, you are too big for our clothes,' she said, and looked away. A friend told me that she once tried to buy some cheese for fondue in a posh fromagerie in Paris and the cheesemonger refused to sell it to her because, in his opinion, it was simply too good to melt for fondue. She had to buy another cheese and tell the cheesemonger that she would use that one for the fondue instead, just so she could buy the cheese that she really wanted.

Anyway, do you want to know what happened to Dad and the steak? Well, I'd love to tell you that he was won over by the chef's skills, that he cut into the juicy steak that was beautifully cooked and just a little pink in the middle, and perfect with the crispy French fries. But that wouldn't be my dad at all; he wanted it charred, carbonized, consumed by fire. He cut off all the bits around the outside, he ate all the fries, he tried a bit of the pink meat, and then a tiny bit more. 'Nope,' he said, 'it's raw in the middle, I'm not a dog, I can't eat that,' before trying just a little more to make sure.

The chef didn't come out to voice his disappointment, but the waiter looked mournful at the meat left on the plate until we left a generous tip and covered the cost of the steak that had been knocked off the bill.

Whenever we go back there, the chef always comes to say hello and to say that he thinks that Dad is probably looking down on us from heaven, shaking his head and barking as we tuck into our pink steaks. He only met my dad once, but he definitely got the measure of him!

Vava's mini steaks and crunchy fries were flawlessly cooked according to every one of us.

'*Mon Dieu,*' remarked Mimi. 'Vava, that's so good – it's bistro cordon bleu.'

'It's a masterpiece,' said Mark.

'Do you like the wine with the steak?' asked Vava.

'Mmm,' said everyone except me. Keen to show I was nearly French, despite arriving at her house bang on time, I quipped, '*C'est le petit Jésus en culotte de velours,*' which roughly translates as 'It's the baby Jesus in velvet pantaloons'. It's an expression I'd learned on my travels and a compliment to be used when wine or food are particularly good!

We each had a small portion of pan-roasted guinea fowl with truffles and leeks, a sliver of monkfish fillet and mussels scented with saffron from Touraine in the Loire Valley, a ragout of clams and some crusty bread to mop up the sauces.

'No cheese tonight, just dessert. I need you to try everything,' said Jacqueline as she brought out a golden tarte Tatin, home-made cinnamon ice cream and pillowy orange soufflé pancakes.

The consensus was that Vava and Jacqueline had

between them cooked a feast that was fit for the gods. We'd all eaten ourselves into pretty much a stupor by the end of the meal, and sat talking in comfortable camaraderie as people who have just bonded over a shared love of food and friends do.

'One day,' said Georges, 'people will flock to your bistro and sing your praises, but we were the first.'

Vava and Jacqueline would make a formidable team. Vava was quiet, sometimes studious, and precise – it was she who prepared the food and her talent was obvious. Jacqueline had an eye for detail and her presentation of the dishes was flawless. She was flirty and loquacious, described by her daughter as the 'perfect hostess who will make everyone feel as if they are VIPs'. 'And she will probably find herself a new husband in the process, with her flirting and giving everyone the eye,' said Vava, knowingly.

'I've had three husbands,' Jacqueline told us. 'You know what they say, if you like something, try it again, three times to be sure and yes, maybe I have time for one more.'

'When you come to Paris next, we must meet up,' she said to me, and I knew I would be in for a different trip from my usual sightseeing dash around the city.

The way that older people are in France is one of the reasons I love it here so much. Mature women in particular are not invisible; they dress and act how they wish, they're not expected to wear homely cardigans and sensible shoes. It's all about being the best you can be for your age, not about dressing as if you're still young. Older women can still do 'the look'. *Le regard* is something particularly French and especially Parisian – I've experienced it a few times myself on the Métro, in bars and on the street.

'*Le regard* is an art, an admiration, it should never be lecherous or make someone uncomfortable,' Vava said, explaining that it's thought the practice came from the Renaissance times and is very clearly an outright appreciation of someone's looks: 'There should be no bumbling Hugh Grant glances.'

I told the story of how a couple of weeks before, on a train heading to the stunning city of Annecy in Haute-Savoie, I'd sat next to a woman and we'd got talking. She was in her mid-seventies and was from Austria. She was on her way to the opera from her home in Paris for she was, she told me, head over heels in love with an opera singer who would be performing in Annecy.

'My husband died seven years ago and I was broken-hearted. I didn't want to live, all the joy had gone from my life. But my daughter took me to the opera house in Vienna to attend a performance of *Carmen*. And he was in the part of Don José, the naive soldier who is seduced and then rejected by Carmen. And he was so beautiful, his voice brought me back to life. I had fallen in love with him by the end of the performance ...' She looked intently at me before carrying on.

'I am seventy-four years old, and I felt that my life was finished, but seeing him gave me a purpose to live, to hear him sing again. So I went to another opera where he was performing. And I told my son and daughter that I had a renewed purpose in life, to follow his performances. I know that it is not a love that will ever be returned. I don't want that. I don't wish to meet him for real, my love is a fantasy. My children don't understand, they say I should see a doctor, that perhaps I'm a little crazy. I moved to Paris three years ago and I live in a tiny flat and my friends here, who are both young and old, think that there is nothing wrong with my dreams. I follow my love's website and when he performs, I take a train to cities and towns all over Europe and I watch him and I'm happy, I'm in love ... maybe I'm a stalker, but I'm happy again.'

'If that was my mother, she would not be watching from the wings. She'd be in there, introducing herself, asking him to dinner,' laughed Vava.

Jacqueline was only a few years younger than the opera-loving lady on the train, but she too was in love with life and ready to start a new career with her daughter, and no one would think her too old, certainly not if they met her.

Mark and I almost rolled home after saying our goodbyes. I promised to catch up with Jacqueline in Paris, since she said she couldn't be tempted to return to the village for a while, not even the following week for an event that Jean-Claude had organized.

189

He had, he said, an idea to hold a snail race. He asked me if I'd ever seen one on any of my travels and I had to admit that I hadn't. I was once invited to participate in a marathon race through the Médoc vineyards of Bordeaux, where people dressed up in wacky costumes (that year the theme was amusement parks). But even more unusually, the marathon includes twenty-three wine stops and *dégustation* (tasting) stops along the route, offering delicacies such as the fattened paunch of pig at the halfway mark and Cap Ferret oysters at the 38-kilometre stage, and as you approach the 39-kilometre point you'll spot a roadside sign of a cow – but don't make the mistake of thinking it's an indication of a cattle grid: it means that there are steaks on offer! Spectators thrust cheese and ice-cream cornets at you and cups of Lillet, a fruit liqueur made close by in Podensac.

A man dressed as candy floss gave me some advice before we started: 'Eating a cork a day keeps the doctor away.' I think he was joking, and I felt I might be hallucinating when a ringmaster and a clown ran past me pursued by Asterix the Gaul. Let me tell you, no number of cheese-and-wine parties prepare you for this event. The victor wins their weight in wine. Me? I've got as much chance of flying to the moon by flapping my arms as winning a marathon, but I'm thinking of tackling a half-marathon in the Marne Valley, Champagne, which offers glasses of champagne instead of water. There's also a foie gras marathon. And for the really foolhardy, there's even a race where you run up the 1,665 steps of the Eiffel Tower. A snail race sounded infinitely less frenetic. Jean-Claude explained how the process would work.

Entrants would turn up with their critters, which are easily found in the garden, and those who arrived snail-less could borrow one from Jean-Claude as he was guaranteed to have plenty. He would charge an entry fee of 2 euros, which included a drink, and the winner pockets all the cash. He had a secret weapon: a snail that was the racing champion of the gastropod world.

The snails would don their racing stripes (a removable sticker applied to their back), before being placed in the middle of the table. The quickest to reach the edge of the table would be the winner. Jean-Claude had been reading about the World Snail Racing Championships in the Gers region, which was too far for him to travel to, so he wanted to start his own Seven Valleys Snail Racing Contest.

'What table?' demanded Bernadette, during the pre-event discussions. 'I'm not having snail slime on my table.'

Jean-Claude looked my way.

'Nor me,' I said hastily.

I had interviewed a British snail farmer a while before, near the town of Hénin-Beaumont, and he'd informed me that snail slime is a common ingredient in modern cough mixtures (yes, really), and encouraged me to lick the undercarriage of a snail just as our ancestors apparently used to do to cure coughs. Apparently, they would also rub snails over wounds to speed up healing. Hmm. I wasn't won over, despite the farmer's demonstration with a snail that he had plucked from its happy place under a leaf in a wild meadow, which he enthusiastically rubbed over his extended tongue. I hadn't given in then and I wasn't keen on having slime-covered furniture now.

I will never understand the obsession that the French have with consuming snails. But the farmer had told me that they've been a popular food since the first days of humanity. Up to the fourteenth century, there were some who thought that snails were in league with the Devil 'because they had no legs and were close to the ground', so the Church forbade the eating of them. But, easy to find and free, snails, as well as frogs' legs, formed a major part of the daily diet of the poorest in France, and when famine struck, the Church relented – though it insisted that the snail be 'purged of its sins'. It was decided that the way to do this was to make the snail 'spit', which was done by sprinkling salt on them, causing the snail to create mucus as a defence mechanism. I like to imagine cardinals, bishops and priests sitting round a long table in a Gothic cathedral, sipping wine out of golden goblets, discussing how to cure a sinful snail. It's that high-value spit that's used in medicines by pharmaceutical companies today, and it's also gaining popularity in skincare.

The French have never lost their love for eating snails. Usually served smothered in a garlic sauce, you can hardly taste the snail at all – which for me is no bad thing. You can feast on snail tikka masala (invented by that British snail farmer in France) and even snail cake, which I had the misfortune to bite into after hearing the words *gâteau moelleux* (which translates as 'soft cake' and doesn't mention 'snail' at all) during a visit to Dijon Market. I didn't see the little eye-stalks sticking out of the slice I was given until it was too late. Snails go on the list of French things that I tried to like but couldn't. This also includes crow pâté (Jean-Claude's 'speciality') and *tête de veau*. The French don't waste any part of a cow and in this hugely popular dish, the brain of a cow is mixed with hard-boiled egg yolks, mustard and oil.

It's said that the French eat a whopping 25,000 tonnes of escargots per annum. Considered the epitome of festive foods at Christmas, alongside oysters they're also served year-round on menus everywhere, sold in jars, in the frozen-food section of supermarkets and at snail farm shops, of which in my part of France there are a surprisingly large number. People will travel for miles to get them fresh or prepared a certain way, such as in a sausage or tart. Just don't take a live snail home on the train with you without a ticket though – in 2008, a Frenchman was fined for doing just this, as the snail was considered a domestic animal. At least the man didn't have to slug it out with SNCF, the railway services, as thankfully they waived the fine.

'I think a snail race is a good idea. The slowest sport in the world – starring the sensational Seven Valleys Snails,' Mark said, encouragingly. 'It's certainly got a ring to it, hasn't it?'

He agreed to make a small round table for the occasion. I think it may even win the title for shortest racetrack in the world at just 45 centimetres from the centre to the edge.

'My snail can do that in about four minutes,' boasted Jean-Claude. He had his eye on the prize, but it was the glory of owning a winning thoroughbred mollusc that really got his imagination running wild.

Race day dawned, overcast and a little drizzly: perfect conditions for snails. The table was carried out to the village green where a poster had been put up a week before advertising the occasion. It even got a mention in the local newspaper: a photo of Jean-Claude, puffed up with importance, holding a jar filled with lettuce and also, apparently, a snail, though you couldn't see it. The story must have been well circulated because on the big day a surprising number of people turned up to take part. In fact, there were so many that the race had to be split into two timed heats. After a long and largely incomprehensible (to us) speech from Jean-Claude, who, overexcited at the unexpectedly good turnout, lapsed into full-on Ch'ti and got distracted when more cars kept arriving.

The contestants for the first round were released from their respective stables, including jam jars and old tobacco tins. One person even had a shoe box complete with windows cut out, but discovered that the snail had escaped on the way to the race. Jean-Claude saved the day by providing a backup snail that had been sourced, along with several others, from my garden the day before. 'You could start a snail farm yourself with this lot,' he'd said.

'Ready, steady, slow,' I called, having been roped in to referee the match. And they were off. Jean-Claude's snail Sebastien, named after St Sebastien, the patron saint of athletes, was competing in the first heat. A small crowd gathered round urging on their beasts.

Five minutes later, they were still racing. Some were slithering about all over the place; they seemed to have forgotten that they were supposed to be heading for the edge. Others, including Sebastien, had refused to come out of their shells.

'*Allez*, *allez*, go, go,' shouted Jean-Claude, but Sebastien was unmoved by the drama.

'You're for the pot,' threatened Jean-Claude, frowning at the reluctant participant who refused to be roused from his slumbers, but his warning had no impact.

The victor, Le Petit Prince, romped home in a little over ten minutes. It was owned by a gleeful four-year-old girl, whose mother had brought her face-painting kit with her, thus ensuring that all the kids were sporting tiger and monkey faces. Sebastien remained in his shell even when the race was over, much to Jean-Claude's disgust.

There was a ten-minute break before the next round. Jean-Claude mopped the table, the kids ran around growling and screeching, people admired the village *stade* and chatted animatedly about the race, saying that it should be an annual thing, which pleased Jean-Claude – he could see a chance to redeem himself. 'The first time is always the hardest,' he announced. 'I focused on setting it up instead of training Sebastien.'

Heat two included Mark's snail, which he'd named Roger Bannister. We'd found him that morning, energetically and aggressively chomping away on my baby leeks and copious weeds at a positively sprint-like pace. Alas, poor Roger – he had a lot to live up to with that name and he failed dismally. Going round and round in circles, he eventually snuggled up to another snail and the pair of them came to a standstill, their eye-stalks waving about with slow abandon while they observed the rest of the snails haphazardly slithering about the slippery tabletop. I think it may have been love.

Ten minutes later, a rather lithe snail called Alphonsine – a galloping gastropod named after the owner's *grand-mère*, who, it was said, moved at around the same speed

– was crowned overall winner, beating the first heat's victor, Le Petit Prince, by a full twenty seconds. I can't see snail-racing making the sports channels, but as an exercise in bringing the community together it was a complete success. Alphonsine's owner kindly donated his winnings to the little girl's mum so she could buy some more face paints.

There were kisses and handshakes all round, and everyone vowed to be there the next year. A new tradition had just been born.

CHAPTER 9

Never can say goodbye

RENDEZVOUS OF ALL kinds linger longer in France due to a seeming reluctance to say *au revoir*, whether it's a chance encounter in the street or an organized catch-up. It's a peculiarly French dilemma.

The ethos 'time is money' doesn't apply in France. I read that the average French manager spends more than sixteen years of their life in meetings, which equates to at least 5,844 days or 140,256 hours if you include leap years. *Mon Dieu.* When you think that the average marriage in the US lasts eight years, it's really quite astonishing.

As for administration, France is in a class of its own. I've had to buy two filing cabinets to store all the paperwork that has been generated by various government agencies over the last few years. And you need to keep every sheet of paper for years because at some point, someone official is bound to want to see it. Even though things are moving more online in France, you'll frequently be asked for a copy of your tax payments, electricity bill, rates, phone bill, driving licence, birth certificate and marriage certificate. So far I have not been asked for my school report, but it can only be a matter of time.

Mark and I once had a meeting at a bank to each open an account. We filled in form after form and produced numerous pieces of paper as requested. The manager asked for more documents than we had brought with us, so we booked another appointment. We returned with the additional paperwork and filled in yet more forms. The manager typed in all the details and questioned us further. In total, it took some three hours before he finally announced that our accounts 'appeared to be in the process of being opened, but don't hold your breath – head office might ask for more paperwork'.

And worse still, since the French think that being positive in formal meetings is not a good thing, they are also generally far from fun. They are serious and earnest, and people are keen to find fault. Negativity is nurtured when it comes to an official rendezvous. It doesn't do to smile too much or be overly enthusiastic: it creates the suspicion that you might be hiding something. And it's not just me who thinks that. A French commercial network that provides information for potential business partners in foreign countries wrote a helpful booklet to give their members a better understanding of how to do business with the French. In it they stated that the French 'sometimes disagree for the sake of discussion and to test conviction ... they potentially view humour as lack of seriousness ...' They also noted that: 'Losing one's temper may be seen as a sign of leadership.' I've learned to be positively pessimistic in a meeting, expect the computer to say 'no' and allow just the briefest of smiles if it doesn't.

And, whatever you do, *never* tell a French person you are excited about a job – or anything else for that matter. It's not that there isn't excitement to be had at a meeting in France, but the word 'excited' simply doesn't translate the same way in French.

There are some words that are called *faux amis* or 'false friends' in French – *excité* is one of them. Announce to a French person that you are excited and they will look at you open-mouthed, wide-eyed and quite possibly take a step back, since they will assume that a particular part of your body is excited rather than your state of mind …

When I visited the town of Orange in Provence a few years ago, I had been blissfully unaware of the dangers of this French word. Orange is famous for its Roman ruins and in particular a first-century AD Roman theatre. In front of rows of stone benches capable of seating 9,000 people, a vast open stage is backed by a 37-metre-high wall topped by a statue of the Roman Emperor Augustus. As a surprise, my friend who worked at the tourist office organized for me to climb the wall to meet the Emperor. How was he to know that I am terrified of heights? On my fortieth birthday, Mark took me to New York City to see the sights and I crawled around the Empire State Building viewing platform on my hands and knees in fear, watched by a bemused and highly entertained group of pensioners on a weekend jolly from Connecticut. (I know this because I heard one say: 'That's not something you see every day in Connecticut. Wait till I tell the folks back home. Quick, take a photo before she crawls back through the door.') Actually, they were quite nice to me. Several asked if I was okay, unlike Mark who thought I was being ridiculous to worry that I could be blown off the top of the Empire State Building over the high wire fencing.

When you visit the Roman theatre at Orange and you're sitting on the benches looking at the stage, you can't see it but behind that stony, time-ravaged exterior and built into the wall is a skinny building with uneven stone stairs that lead to the top. Carved away by time and years of sandalled Roman feet in places, worn and crumbling in others, some of the steps were so steep that I had to literally pull myself up them as if I were climbing a tree. Onwards and upwards, round and round we went. Through dusty antechambers and along cramped corridors, across planks of wood with deep chasms below. Eventually, we emerged onto a platform right behind the famous statue of Emperor Augustus. I was dishevelled and red-faced on account of the August midday temperature hovering somewhere around the boiling point of blood, but thrilled all the same.

'You made a lot of squeaks,' my friend said, as we

stood looking down at pin-sized people aiming their cameras at the statue with no idea that we were standing behind him. 'Are you okay?'

'I was afraid,' I said, 'but very excited.' This caused him to go even redder than me, and I noticed that on the way back he didn't offer to hold my hand to help me down as he had on the journey up.

It wasn't until we'd made it through to the cheese course – a deliciously soft and creamy Saint-Marcellin drizzled with honey – at dinner in La Grotte d'Auguste restaurant, which is built into a Roman wall near the theatre, that he asked if I knew what I'd be writing about my visit and went on to explain that I'd told him I was aroused by reaching the Emperor. I nearly spat my cheese out, but two faux pas in one day would have been a bit much.

It's not just business meetings that can go on for longer than you ever thought possible. When we have dinner with French friends, we feel as if we almost have to train before the event. Early nights in the week leading up to it, fasting during the day itself and committing to a time to leave. Don't get me wrong, it's not because our French friends are boring. They're not. Some of them are downright fascinating. Take Gaspard, Gary and Annette's neighbour. He invited us to dinner as a thank-you for helping him to chop down a tree in his garden which, thanks to a particularly powerful storm, had fallen over the top of one of his wells.

In the gloomy room, lit by a single bare light bulb and a couple of oil lamps, we could see pots bubbling on every hob of the wood-fired oven and the air was filled with steam and scintillating smells. Gary and Annette were seated on one side of the long table in the centre of the room, Mark and I were sat opposite, and Gaspard was perched on a stool at one end of the table. Gaston the parakeet was in his cage, speaking mostly incomprehensible French, though every now and again we could clearly make out some swear words.

'I had to put him in his bed,' said Gaspard, 'as he, like me, is a food critic, and he will want to taste a little of everything from all of us and if he doesn't like it he will bite you.'

'*Merde*,' screamed Gaston, as his sharp claws wound around the bars of his cage and he stared with unblinking eyes.

'*Oh là là*,' remarked the bird, as Gaspard brought in a tray of whole roasted garlic bulbs. The papery skins had been cut halfway up and 'smeared with salty Breton butter, seasoned and slowly baked for two hours', in Gaspard's words, until they were golden and soft. Spread over pieces of his home-baked bread, it was a heavenly amuse-bouche, which roughly translates as 'mouth amuser' – a small bite of something to get your juices flowing. It's a particularly French custom; restaurants often provide a complimentary, dainty amuse-bouche to show creativity.

'*Oooo jolie*,' screeched Gaston as cheese-and-ham-filled éclairs, with just a hint of cinnamon, were presented.

Dinner consisted of a pie filled with chicken and salsify (a sort of skinny white parsnip that tastes a little like oysters), which earned the sound of kisses from the gourmet bird.

Dessert was a dish that I recognized from my trip to Gascony: an Armagnac-flavoured apple pie topped with wafer-thin, scrunched-up filo pastry, which gives the dish its name: *croustade* (crusty).

Gaston actually managed to look sad and said softly what sounded like '*Mais je t'aime, ma chérie*' ('But I love you, darling').

We were oblivious to the bird; the food was so wonderful that his cravings were nothing to us.

A mobile phone rang for a few seconds and then stopped abruptly. 'It's mine,' said Gaspard, jumping up from the table. 'Perhaps it is my girlfriend. We had a fight and she left me. We can't live together, but we can't love apart.'

He looked all around the room for his phone and couldn't find it. Gaspard became panicked, sure that it would be his little *puce*, as he called her, and that he must call her back as soon as possible. A *puce* is a flea, and only in France would a creature that spread the bubonic plague be used as a term of endearment.

Gary rang Gaspard's number, but we couldn't hear it ringing.

'There's a slight glow coming from the room next door,' Annette said, looking at the open door that led to the bedroom.

'*Bah*, it's in the bed!' Gaspard shouted, and dashed in, returning with a look of confusion as he checked the call log.

'Hmm, no missed calls … no *puce* … How strange.'

The ringtone sounded again, but not from the phone – it was the parakeet. We referred to it ever after as Gaston's revenge.

Whenever we go to dinner with French friends and we're ready to leave, I'll look at my watch and say: 'Ooh, is that the time already? We really must make a move.' With fellow British friends we have no such qualms: 'Got to go now,' we say, 'things to do, people to see, places to go in the morning, thanks for a lovely night, see you soon.' We're putting on coats, walking to the door. We leave.

Not so when you're at the home of French people. At this stage you are persuaded a *digestif* is a necessity before you go. Of course it is; alcohol at three o'clock in the morning is always a good idea.

You can't rush a *digestif* either. You must sip and savour it, whether it be Calvados, Cognac, Armagnac or something more exotic like Chartreuse. Legend has it (and who doesn't love a good legend) that the only people who know the recipe and ingredients for the famous fern-green or dandelion-yellow liqueur are two Carthusian monks tucked away in the Grand Chartreuse monastery in Voiron, not far from Grenoble. The monks of Chartreuse have lived their life of self-imposed isolation for more than 900 years. There are twenty-five *chartreuses* (or 'charterhouses' as they are known in English) around the world. Close to where I live, at the foot of the hilltop town of Montreuil-sur-Mer, and somehow hidden among trees and fields, is La Chartreuse de Neuville. It is monumental in size and history and was once on the pilgrimage route. Mary, Queen of Scots allegedly stopped off here in 1561 on her way to Scotland and left with a gift of two peacocks. There are several cloisters, plus chapels and dozens of individual apartments where the brothers would live alone, undisturbed and unknown. Even when they died, they were buried without record, their egos put aside for the sake of humanity.

All Carthusian monks and nuns spend their days listening for God in silent meditation and praying for each of our souls. All the monks, of course, except for the two who brew the Chartreuse, which is made from a whopping 130 local herbs, plants and other botanicals gathered in the local mountains. The monk duo concoct the powerfully alcoholic and throat-burning mixture according to an ancient recipe that was given to their predecessors by an aristocrat named François-Annibal d'Estrées in 1605. It came in the form of a manuscript, of unknown origins, which contained details of all the plants and instructions on how to use them to create an elixir of 'long life'. In *Brideshead Revisited*, Evelyn Waugh wrote that imbibing Chartreuse was akin to drinking the colours of the rainbow: 'It's like swallowing a spectrum.' Mark calls it cough mixture.

So we down the *digestif* carefully and reverently. This is the cue for Mark to say: 'Right, we really must go now.'

'Oh, but coffee is just coming.'

We drink the coffee – we're now ready to run home with our eyes wide open.

'Right,' we say again, fidgeting, slapping thighs, looking at watches, staring at each other with eyes on stalks. We stand to get our coats.

'More coffee?'

'No, no,' we say in unison, 'we really must go. We start work in a few hours.' We grab our coats and walk to the door.

'Are you sure you don't want more coffee? We're having one.'

We smile and leave and wonder about their sleep patterns. The only way we will make it through the working day is by lurching from one cup of coffee to the next. Perhaps they are just starting early?

It's not only saying goodbye to people that's difficult. When you have pets, inevitably the time comes to say goodbye to them, though we didn't know it until it was too late for one of our beloved dogs.

The day started as it normally does. Every morning I

get up first. Mark is not a morning person, whereas I am irritatingly chipper even before the sun is up. I let the cats in and out, get food for the wild birds and wander down to the pens to feed and water the chickens, ducks and geese. I keep my boots in the dogs' room, so I always wander through and say good morning to them before getting Mark up and then walking them together. The dogs sleep in large cages. Bruno the Labrador has one to himself, while Ella Fitzgerald and Churchill share one – they have been inseparable since they were kept together in a glass box in a pet shop when they were puppies. They like their cages; it's their own personal space. We tried leaving them to sleep by the fire in the front room, but they didn't settle: Ella Fitzgerald ate the leather sofa, the TV remote control and munched on the doors, which made it look as if a colossal chipmunk had gone mad and tried to eat the room; Bruno roamed the house looking for food, eating bits of paper and chewing the cushions; Churchill barked to snitch on the others.

Entering the dogs' room is the cue for them to wag their tails like crazy against the metal cages – you can hardly hear yourself think. I talk to them all the time: 'Morning dogs, did you sleep well, are you ready for your walk …' The word 'walk' provokes an even louder din. But that morning was unusually subdued. Churchill and Bruno were standing up and staring out of the cages, wagging their tails but not their usual happy selves. Ella Fitzgerald seemed to be in a deep sleep. She lay on her side in her normal sleep position, her long legs stretched out, a peaceful look on her face. At first I didn't realize what had happened. My brain simply didn't register it.

I once read that grief is love that you can't give to someone. We were heartbroken. She was only ten years old and had seemed as fit as a fiddle. The day before, we'd been for a walk and she'd run ahead of everyone as usual, looking for pheasants under the hedgerows and disturbing owls that were trying to hunt for a last snack before the full light of day sent them off to barns and leafy canopies for a well-earned sleep. She'd posed for a photo, staring into my phone camera, her brown eyes sparkling and her nose shiny and wet.

We buried her under a hazel tree near the chicken pen because she loved to chase them.

Broken hearts aren't just reserved for humans. Bruno had lost his soulmate and pined for weeks. We had to avoid saying her name out loud as he would look around, full of hope. Churchill was quiet for a few days and didn't eat properly for a long time; I would have to stand with him and coax him to swallow some food. In the evenings, the two boys lay on their beds in the front room as all three had always done as Mark and I watched TV or read books. After a while they began to cuddle up together, no longer rivals for the affection of the dog they both loved best.

Our walks have never felt quite the same without her. It quickly became very clear that it was she who led the boys off into the forest to chase deer or pheasants, who started them howling in the garden when they heard a noise and who rummaged in the bins when our backs were turned. She will always have a special place in our hearts.

But life goes on, and later that week I had to travel to Montpellier. I go everywhere by train, usually from Étaples to Paris and onwards, and on this particular early morning drive to Étaples, the wind howled a tormented shriek through the valleys and the sky refused to lighten.

On the way to the train station, we dropped in at a tiny two-pump petrol station. Mark filled the car, and I went into the little shop to pay and was greeted by an old spaniel and a small, ancient sausage dog (a dachshund, to be specific), who dragged themselves out of their beds to come and say hello. A wizened old lady finally appeared from behind a door at the back of the shop and I got a glimpse of what was clearly her sitting room. 'That wind is *soufflé*,' she said. I could only agree as we looked out of the window at the wind whipping the leaves into a frenzied dance, making skinny trees bend over, while a dustbin lid merrily escaped down the road. Then she remarked: '"Love is like the wind – we don't know where it comes from," so said Honoré de Balzac.'

Strangely enough, Claudette had also quoted Balzac the day before. We'd been talking about 'influencers' on social media. Claudette knows that I write, but I was trying to explain to her that I also spend a lot of time chatting to people all around the world on social media channels, and that there are some people who make a fortune from 'influencing' others and they are usually young and beautiful. 'Ah,' she said, 'Balzac wrote that those who have youth and beauty, which are conferred by chance, make some as proud as if they were hard-won.' Well, I certainly can't disagree with her, but how someone aged almost ninety can remember all these quotes I really don't know. I wonder if she has them written in a book somewhere and refreshes her memory several times a day – I know I'd have to! It made me wonder if all elderly French ladies spend their days learning quotes by great French writers.

Arriving in Paris, I hopped on the train from Gare du Nord to get to Gare de Lyon where I'd arranged to meet Jacqueline, Vava's mother, at Le Train Bleu, which is without a doubt one of the poshest train-station buffets in the world. A grand horseshoe-style staircase leads from the station concourse to a sparkling Belle Époque restaurant that looks exactly as it did in 1901 when it first opened. The food is classic French and expensive, but it's worth it just to see the gloriously exuberant décor with lavishly painted frescoes, glittering chandeliers and lots of gold-coloured woodwork. It's the Versailles of train-station restaurants.

Jacqueline and I had become friends via email since meeting at Vava's house. Her long rambling messages were similar to her conversation style: slightly eccentric, irreverent and insightful. I asked her if my neighbours' liberal use of witty and poignant sayings was a *thing*.

'Yes, indeed,' she replied, laughing. 'We French love our quotes, especially if they are from classical literature or history. It makes us look a lot smarter, more sophisticated and better educated than we really are – I include myself in that bag! If you can quote the ancients, and especially foreign writers or poets, you will really win your fellows' admiration despite not speaking or understanding a single word of those languages. I personally like to quote Oscar Wilde quite liberally to impress my friends, but also because I think he is wonderful and we are proud he lived with us in France.'

The playwright had spent time in Paris, where there was a more laissez-faire attitude and his lifestyle wasn't judged so harshly. Alas, he died in poverty in what was then the seedy (now splendidly luxurious) Hôtel d'Alsace on rue des Beaux-Arts. As he lay dying in his hotel room, he uttered what some say were his final words: 'My wallpaper and I are fighting a duel to the death. One or the other of us has to go.'

Jacqueline and I chatted as if we had known each other for years while the waiters performed a choreographed dash from table to table, coddling the regulars, carving the meat at the table, pouring wine deftly and never spilling a drop, making tourists feel chic (or not). We could hear the muffled sounds of station announcements and the whoosh of engines as trains came and went.

'I sometimes come here just to people-watch,' Jacqueline said. On the banquette next to us, an elderly man sat alone studying a copy of *Le Figaro*, a glass of red wine before him. A couple on the other side of us were talking animatedly and taking photos of crêpes Suzette being flambéed before their eyes. It would be easy to sit here all afternoon, but I had a date with an art museum in Montpellier, one of my favourite cities in France.

Jacqueline and I said our goodbyes and I boarded a train bound for southern France. I arrived in Montpellier in time for dinner and to watch the sun set over the Gothic Cathedral Saint-Pierre. If I was to live in a city, which I am not sure is now possible with the number of animals I currently have, Montpellier would definitely be a contender. It's arty and architecturally thrilling, with a medieval old town featuring a warren of cobbled streets that are edged by a 'newer' district lined with grand eighteenth-century buildings. Beyond those well-established areas lies the exciting new Antigone neighbourhood, which has buildings created by the world's most innovative architects. It's also close enough to hop on a tram (decorated with designs by none other than French fashion designer Christian Lacroix) to gorgeous Mediterranean beaches. And in the centre of it all is the monumental city square – Place de la Comédie, the largest pedestrian square in Europe. Or, as the locals call it, Place de l'Œuf – Egg Square – on account of its oval shape. It's perfect for sitting at a café, sipping an aperitif and watching the world of Montpellier pass by, including buskers and breakdancers, old ladies with shopping trolleys heading to market, suited and booted men, chic women, children shrieking to go on the carousel and oodles of students, who have been drawn to this historic centre of learning which is home to one of the oldest universities in France, established in 1220.

Two days later, while stopping off at the *toilettes* at Gare du Nord on my way home, the lady who works there said '*bonjour*', which stopped me in my tracks because normally she's not very friendly. The women who manage public toilets in France generally command more respect than they might in other countries. They've been affectionately nicknamed 'Dame Pipi', and in their domain they are the bosses of the WCs of swanky hotels and large restaurants, train stations and public facilities in big cities. Sadly, these types of conveniences are gradually being replaced with terrifying pop-up toilets whose doors slam behind you and you start thinking you're never going to get out and the *pompiers* will have to come and rescue you – either that or they open unexpectedly and disgorge you onto the street.

I travel through Gare du Nord often and always say '*bonjour*' to Dame Pipi as she sits in the doorway inspecting those who enter, as well as those who pass by, with a sometimes-inscrutable look; occasionally she makes it obvious that she's unimpressed. She wields her mop like a weapon, glaring at anyone who dares to tread where she has cleaned. The last time I'd been there, she was holding court with the other Dame Pipis, moaning about having to clear up 'the shit of the whole world' and at that very moment I walked past. We locked eyes and I said, '*Merci Madame,*' and she just nodded slowly to me. Of all the things that have made me feel that I may at last be becoming acceptably almost French, being acknowledged by a Dame Pipi in Paris comes somewhere near the top.

And then something happened that made me feel very un-French. On the train journey home from Paris to Lille, before heading on to Saint-Omer, there was a problem halfway down the line and all the trains were halted. Our train was stopped at a town in the middle of nowhere just after five o'clock. We sat there for an hour and then the train driver announced we would all have to get off and wait outside the station. I lugged my case off and followed the other passengers out into the street to await further news. There were just a few houses in the small town, and nowhere to sit and wait. Another hour passed before an SNCF (train company) official arrived; we knew it must be bad if he'd been despatched to talk to us rather than the train driver.

'The problem on the line is serious,' he announced solemnly, 'and there is no possibility of trains resuming tonight.' There was a collective groan – Saint-Omer was still some 50 kilometres away.

'Don't worry, we're organizing taxis from all around to take you on to Saint-Omer and to stop at any stations en route,' the official explained, reassuringly. 'Of course, you will not have to pay.' All well and good, these things happen. But then he went on to say: 'Taxis will all depart at the same time, as if you were on the train: no one will be getting preferential treatment over anyone else. There will be four passengers to a taxi. It could take some time to organize for all of you. Please come one at a time to tell me what station you want.'

By that point, several people had already left, having called for someone to come and collect them, and many more began to reach for their mobile phones to make alternative arrangements. That left around fifty of us still to get to Saint-Omer, including me, as although Mark was picking me up from the station, he'd forgotten to take his phone and I couldn't let him know where I was or what was happening.

We continued to sit in the street for hours and the day turned to night. Taxis started to arrive in dribs and drabs and they sat there too. There was a little grumbling, but no one argued with the fact that it was only fair that we all went together: *liberté, égalité, fraternité* and all that. It was after midnight by the time they had enough taxis to fit us all in and we arrived at Saint-Omer around an hour later. Mark was waiting in the car park – he'd seen the notices in the station so he was aware of the situation. We were both dumbfounded at the fact that everyone had accepted the 'all for one and one for all' approach to managing the onward journey. If that had been the UK, at best they would have drawn straws to get in the cars and move on, and at worst there'd have been punch-ups.

Back on the home front, it was hedge-cutting time again. Our garden had once been two fields of a farm that had belonged to Claudette's family, and although the smelly sheep we inherited with the garden was long gone, the hedges remained from the old days of more than a hundred years ago. The trees had grown so tall that they now obscured the upstairs windows of Claudette's house. She said that she didn't mind; at her age, she doesn't climb the stairs anymore and all the things she needs are on the ground floor.

'Victor Hugo said that forty is the old age of youth and fifty is the youth of old age – I'm not sure what he'd say about me,' remarked Claudette when I popped round to let her know we were in hedge-chopping mode.

'Yoko Ono says some people are old at eighteen and some are young at ninety,' I replied. That pleased her a great deal.

The sun had finally come after what had felt like weeks of non-stop ferocious rainfall. The farmers' fields were claggy and some of them had turned into impromptu ponds. Alongside meadow flowers suddenly bursting into bloom, the weeds had reached gargantuan heights. By the way, did you know that the word 'gargantuan' comes from the book *Gargantua*, which was written in the sixteenth century by Frenchman François Rabelais? It tells the fascinating life story of a voracious giant.

Even Bread Man remarked on the size of the weeds in my garden. Writer A. A. Milne of *Winnie-the-Pooh* fame once said: 'Weeds are flowers too, once you get to know them.' I'm sorry, Mr Milne, but I have to disagree – the weeds in my garden are monstrously huge and meddlesome. But one thing I have learned about country life is that you have to look for silver linings, and at least the bees love the flowering weeds.

Bread Man didn't just drop off one loaf of bread that day as he usually does. He handed me several days' worth, explaining that he wouldn't be able to deliver at the weekend on account of a rally car race being held in these parts. Each year, rally drivers turn up from all over to race their very expensive cars from swanky Le Touquet, a seaside town known as the Monaco of the north. They dart up and down hills, bolt round hairpin bends and scoot through the little villages of the Seven Valleys, before returning to Le Touquet for champagne and celebrations.

'You should take part yourself,' I suggested, as he stood cuddling Tigger the spoiled cat, who had come stalking through the jungle of weeds like a tiny tiger, peering at us and purring when she saw him. She knows that he thinks she is the best thing since sliced bread.

I liked the idea of Bread Man, with his twinkly eyes,

twirly moustache and blue cloth cap pulled down firmly over his unruly dark hair, sitting hunched over the steering wheel of his little bread van, taking on the precious rally cars – and winning by a mile.

CHAPTER 10

It's not what you say but the way that you say it

'WHAT IS THE word for "zoo" in English?' asked Bread Man as two cats wandered past my front door. Shadow the black cat had her tongue hanging out as usual, while neurotic Winston studiously ignored us. The dogs were barking in the garden exchanging news with other dogs in the village, and two vocal chickens sat on chairs on the terrace, almost as if they were expecting a waiter to come over to take their order. Three chickens were perched on a ledge, peering through the front-room windows, while further down the garden yet more chickens ran amok with the ducks and geese.

'Zoo,' I answered.

'*Non*,' he said in a tone of disbelief, much like when he asked me what the English word is for 'croissant'.

'No,' I replied.

'Eh?'

'It's not *non*, it's "no". And *oui*, it really is zoo, the same!'

I was waiting for him to ask what the English word for 'voyeur' was, as he considered the leering window-peeping chickens. But we were distracted by the arrival of Tigger the cat, a ball of white fluff with grey patches on her head and back, and grey stripes on one leg. '*Oulà, le Sergent-Major*,' said Bread Man.

I am frequently amazed at just how many words are almost the same in French as in English. The problem lies in how we interpret the saying of the words. I used to laugh at my dad's attempts to speak French, which mainly consisted of talking very loudly in English with a French accent, but in fairness he often came quite close. Some estimates claim that more than 30 per cent of English words are the same or similar in French, we just say them differently.

I'll be honest, I've not found it easy to learn to speak French. I had schoolgirl French when I came here, and after years of practice I can understand the language well enough to interview people, read a newspaper, watch a film and follow the news, and I can even read French books. But even after all this time, I still struggle with the dreaded grammar.

French language isn't just about words, phrases and grammar, though, or whether to use *tu* or *vous*, *on* or *nous*. And it's not just about knowing the words for everything, which is impossible since new words are constantly being created. The French dictionary Le

Petit Larousse considers 1,000 candidates for inclusion every year. Lexicology fans eagerly await the details of new words. Judging is strict. The term must be frequently used. There must be no technical jargon. Words must be democratically employed; this is France, after all. Any words that are a fad and likely to disappear as rapidly as they appeared will not be considered. Only a handful make the cut, and words that go out of fashion are ruthlessly eliminated. It's an observation of French society in its own way, as the words tend to reflect what's been going on in the lives of the country's citizens. These are not just empty words. Take '*smicardisation*', which is when a company or body pays the bulk of employees the minimum basic wage, and is often shortened to just '*smic*'. Then there's '*slasheur*' – someone who does several jobs and/or activities at the same time. Traditionally in France, young people choose a career path early in life and, in the past, they tended to stick to it. For me, it really reflects a change in the French mindset, particularly among young people.

The highly influential Académie française also publishes a dictionary. Created in 1634 by none other than Cardinal Richelieu, the academy functions to ensure that the French language is 'pure and comprehensible by all'. Essentially, it is a sort of language police department. Its dictionary is exceptionally highbrow and takes years to be updated from one version to the next. The ninth edition, for example, has been in progress since 1986.

To make it even more challenging to learn French, a lot of words have several definitions: *baguette*, for instance, doesn't just refer to a long skinny loaf, but to almost anything that is long and straight – so it also means 'wand', 'baton' and 'stick'. *Baguettes* is also slang for 'skinny legs', and your hair can be as straight as baguettes. A magic wand is a *baguette magique*, and a handbag that you hold under your arm can be called a *baguette* (in acknowledgement of the way that the French carry their bread). Context is very important when speaking French.

Plus, there are some words which are so peculiarly French that there is simply no equivalent in English, like *terroir* which is used to describe the circumstances in which, for example, vines grow, based on the local soil, weather and several other things. Or *flâneur*: someone who likes to stroll just for the sake of it.

Talking French is about body language too – think of shoulder shrugs, eye rolls and hand gestures. And blowing raspberries. And other strange noises: *houp-là* (whoops), *pfff* (sigh), *oulà* (wow, in a good way) and *oh là là* (wow, in a negative way). Occasionally it's *oh là là là là là là* – then you know it's *really* serious.

Mark, who is deaf in one ear, has also struggled to learn French, but he understands it better than he speaks it. He gets by, though, and frequently has entire conversations with Jean-Claude where the only words he uses are *oui*, *non* and *ça va*, which means both 'how are you?' and 'I'm okay'.

Take the time when we heard some urgent knocking at our front door. I knew it was urgent because, living in the middle of nowhere, we don't get many people coming to the front. Neighbours and friends tend to wander through the gate, which is clearly marked *ATTENTION AU CHIEN* – beware of the dog. They take no notice of the sign and just carry on round to the back of the house and enter through the kitchen. Even the man who comes to read the water meter, which is down a hole in my hall, heads round the back and yells for us to let him in.

Most of the time I love this informality, although there have been occasions when it has bugged me – like when I'm concentrating really hard in the garden. One time I was sowing lettuce seeds, trying to get them in a straight line, not too deep. I was smiling away to myself, imagining the large plump lettuces that we would enjoy, when I started to feel uneasy. I shrugged off the feeling and moved along, mumbling to myself. After several minutes I stood up to stretch my legs and gasped when I saw one of my neighbours just standing there, watching.

'How long have you been there?' I asked.

'A long time, but I didn't like to disturb you,' said the neighbour. I must admit it freaked me out a little bit.

The insistent knocking at the door was Jean-Claude,

breathless and pink with excitement, saving time by not going round to the back of the house.

'*Bonjour!*' said Jean-Claude. (Even in an emergency you have to say '*bonjour*' – it is the law in France.) 'Have you heard about the hydrangea problem?'

'*Non*,' I replied.

'Really? You haven't heard? Well, pour me a glass of wine and I will tell you what's been going on.'

He came in, settled down in a chair and made himself comfortable as I pulled the cork and called out to Mark to come in from the workshop where he was making wardrobe doors.

'*Ça va?*' Jean-Claude asked Mark.

'*Ça va. Ça va?*'

'*Ça va, ça va.* You'll never guess. Someone has stolen my hydrangea heads.'

What can you say to that except '*non*' in a tone of disbelief?

'And it's not just me. It's all over the news, even on the telly. Hydrangea thieves in this area. They've been nicking the flowers, drying the petals and smoking them.'

He looked at us expectantly, but I had no idea how to reply and neither did Mark. I blew a raspberry and gave a Gallic shrug of solidarity.

'You know what it means, don't you?'

'*Non.*'

'I phoned the *gendarmes* about it, but they said they had better things to do. Can you believe that?'

'*Oui.*' I could actually believe that, while Mark made a '*Pfff*' sound and rolled his eyes to indicate disgust.

'Anyway, I'm going to be keeping an eye out in the village. I'll be patrolling the streets where there are hydrangeas. I don't think it's anyone from round here, so if you see anything strange can you come and tell me so I can check it out?'

'*Oui,*' we said, because it seemed to be the right answer.

'You speak such great French these days,' said Jean-Claude. Okay, maybe he didn't actually say that, but if you asked him how that conversation went, he would see absolutely nothing wrong with it and would most likely say that we had a perfectly acceptable chat in French. He finished his wine and dashed off to tell someone else the news. Much later, Bernadette confessed that she had in fact pruned the hydrangeas, but didn't have the heart to tell her excitable husband.

Small villages are a hotbed of gossip and tittle-tattle is to be shared like a fine wine. And when most of the time nothing much happens, you make the best of what you have. So when five life-sized plastic Jersey cows appeared on a nearby traffic roundabout, it caused a bit of a stir. Were they there for the benefit of drivers? Or to amuse the real cows in the fields on either side of the road, like pretend friends? The French are obsessed with roundabouts: almost a third of all the traffic roundabouts in the world are to be found in France. In fact, the first one ever was constructed in Paris, at the Place de l'Étoile (Star Square) – now called Place Charles de Gaulle – on which sits the Arc de Triomphe and where a nightmarish twelve avenues converge. It's said that if you're involved in an accident driving round the circle, the insurance companies split the cost fifty-fifty as each driver is considered at fault. Allegedly, it's the only place in the city where an accident is not judged. I've never driven in this part of Paris and I doubt I ever will.

Town councils love to put things on roundabouts. I've seen them covered in model villages, incredible floral displays, giant snails, wine bottles, enormous plastic hands and bizarre art installations. Occasionally, *gilets jaunes* (yellow-vested protesters) have been spotted having a picnic on them while they take a break from getting their message across.

Driving in France can be quite an odd experience at times. There's the *priorité à droite* rule for starters – this means that drivers entering a road from the right, even onto a main road, have priority and you have to stop and let them out. But not at a roundabout. In that situation, those coming from the left have priority. And it's not on all roads, only where there's a sign for *priorité à droite*, which makes it even more hazardous as it's so random. Some French drivers see it as a test of will to utilize this crazy law without stopping or looking, which doesn't always get good results; it's just as tricky for the French as it is for foreign drivers. The French government has introduced a programme to phase it out, though where

I live, it's not obvious. There are still dozens of sneaky roads allowing this practice and even when the road rule is updated, local drivers invariably ignore it because they don't think the rule should have been changed. I assure you, though, the hand gestures used in the UK when communicating in such circumstances appear to be just as well understood in France.

Some transport laws are even more odd. For instance, in the lovely wine-making area of Châteauneuf-du-Pape in Provence, where the Popes of Avignon built their summer residence back in 1320 (who can blame them?), a law was passed by the mayor in the 1950s making it illegal to fly a UFO over the town. That law is still valid to this day, and it seems to work, since no one has ever spotted aliens in the skies above the vineyards there.

'Do they have plastic cows on the roundabouts in Paris?' asked Arnaud the barman, when Mark and I were in the local bar for our usual end-of-the-week aperitifs. 'You go there a lot – have you seen any?'

'No, I can't say I have ever seen a plastic cow on a traffic circle in Paris.'

The locals generally feel that Paris is a different country to the rest of France and that Parisians are not like the rest of the French.

'They have a restaurant in Paris where everyone eats in the nude, you know,' said Monsieur Martel, a seventy-something widower, who has been wooing Madame Bernadette for the past ten years. 'Apparently the staff are dressed, for hygiene reasons, but the guests are as naked as the day they were born.'

'Have you ever been there?' Arnaud asked me, and everyone stopped talking to listen in, keen for a bit of gossip.

I've heard of this restaurant but I wasn't tempted, even though their coq au vin was said to be rather good. I also wasn't tempted to go to a Paris theatre performance in which the actors were all naked – as was the entire audience – and nor was I tempted by a naked museum visit (the Palais de Tokyo tickets sold out for that exhibition).

'Erm, *non*,' I replied, after a pause. They all looked crestfallen; it would have been a great bit of gossip.

'D'you think we would get away with it here?' Monsieur Martel asked, chortling.

'*Non*, I'd have to put the heating on all day and it's expensive enough as it is,' said Arnaud, who is notorious for his frugality.

Some would have you believe that all the French are into flinging off their clothes and going topless on beaches at the drop of a hat. Not in the north they're not, that's for sure, though there are a couple of naturist beaches along the Opal Coast, which have very prominent signs to ensure that no one inadvertently wanders onto them. It happened to me once in the south. I went camping with a friend many years ago. We drove around the coast of France from Calais to Bordeaux. We veered away from the larger towns and the more well-known areas, discovering little villages, gorgeous local cafés and stunning landscapes. In the evenings we'd find somewhere to camp, which was never a problem as long as we turned up in reasonable time to book, pay and pitch our tent.

One night we were late in locating a place to stay after roaming around the beautiful Médoc Atlantique area, and it was a huge relief when the car headlamps picked out a sign for a campsite 15 kilometres away. It was almost midnight by the time we arrived and we were exhausted. It was dark on the approach to the small reception hut where a man leaned out of the window and told us how lucky we were to get in as he was just off to bed. He took our money, gave us a map of the campsite and pointed us in the direction of where we could set up camp.

We put the tent up in the pitch-black with only a piddly little torch providing any light. It was very quiet apart from the noise that we were making, and we finally got in our sleeping bags and fell into a deep sleep.

The heat of the morning sun woke us up even though it was early. We opened the flap of the tent and just lay there dozing, relaxed and enjoying the start of yet another beautiful summer's day in south-west France. The smell of pine trees was strong; we could hear cicadas making their distinctive wee-wee-wee noise. Legend has it that they were sent by God to sabotage the peasants' endless siestas and stop them from getting too lazy in the sunny south.

A pretty good choice for a campsite considering it was so last-minute, we thought. The man who welcomed us the night before had told us we were right next to a beach resort called Le Gurp. The sound of the waves was audible and there was a light breeze: it was glorious. Then something pink flashed across the front of the tent.

People were starting to wake up on the campsite. We could hear low voices, pans being clanked, the smell of gas as camping stoves were being lit. Then, another pink flash in front of the tent doors ... it looked like ... a person cartwheeling ... in the nude – *quelle surprise!*

I pulled myself up off the floor and got out of the sleeping bag, wearing my pyjamas, and climbed out of the tent. All around me were naked people. A lady at the pitch next door was bent over a fire stirring a pot – it was a stirring sight, I can tell you. A man on a bike was wearing just a bumbag (or fanny pack, if you're American). A group of elderly ladies and gents carrying tennis rackets came by talking animatedly in German, in the nude – giving a whole new meaning to the term 'ball boys'. Of course – it was a naturist camping site; we'd been so tired that we'd missed that bit when we booked in.

Le Gurp itself was lovely. The beach was fabulous with golden sands and pine trees, half-buried bunkers littered the shore, shallow waters made it a surfers' paradise and wonderful restaurants served great platters of fresh seafood.

The naturist campers were unselfconscious and for the most part getting on a bit – a mix of Dutch, German and French mostly. It was a little disconcerting at first to go into the campsite shop and see so many naked people queuing at the meat counter, and I couldn't bring myself to hire a bike or a pedalo, but the bare truth is that for a great all-over tan, it certainly takes some beating.

After regaling our friends with tales of the naturist campsite, Mark and I left the bar to head home, leaving the regulars disappointed in my lacklustre attitude towards the decadent pleasures of Paris, but amused by my accidental foray into a nudist colony. It was a typically wet spring evening; the fields were saturated and rivulets of rainwater flowed down hilly roads, while low clouds hid the tops of the electricity-producing windmills that are appearing in an ever-larger number in the area. The wind buffeted our car and lightning flashed across the sky. When we got home we discovered that the power was down, and it stayed that way for the whole night and into the next morning.

We played cards by candlelight in front of a roaring wood fire and talked about the 'good old days', when people didn't have the internet or mobile phones. Once, we'd had a power cut when one of our kids was staying and she was quite bereft without access to the web. We, however, having a home here with snail-like internet speed and no mobile signal at all for fourteen years, are quite able to cope with the consequences of no internet without going stir-crazy (at least for a few hours). If you live in rural France, you had better get used to power cuts when the weather is wild. The electric cables are overhead, so all it takes is a tree to come down somewhere for everything to grind to a halt. It's such a normal part of life for country folk that it's considered a mishap rather than a calamity.

Claudette is nonplussed by the fuss when the lights go off. She has lived through many times when the power would be out for long periods. Like us, she doesn't have central heating and relies on a wood fire. She doesn't possess a computer or any kind of mobile device. Her TV is very old and she mostly watches programmes in black and white, unperturbed by the poor quality of the images. The only time she insists it's in colour and shows a clear picture is when a royal wedding is on; then she'll go to her daughter's house at the bottom of the hill. Claudette adores the British royal family, and judging by the amount of coverage they get in French newspapers and magazines, plenty of the French are fascinated by them. The Queen, of course, is their favourite, neither snobby nor authoritarian and always unruffled. Claudette reckons Her Majesty would cope quite well with a power cut too: 'She'd get out the candles. Then you can read, you can write, you can see the person next to you. You can cook on the oven and pour a glass of wine. *Après la pluie, le beau temps.*' This well-known phrase literally translates as 'After the rain, nice weather', or, as we say in English, 'Every cloud has a silver lining'.

The power came on in the early hours of the morning, making the alarm clock flash and the freezer temperature monitor bleep. After breakfast we nipped next door to see if Claudette needed anything and discovered that, yet again, one of our cockerels was getting up to mischief. Roger Moore, the dad of Reggie and Ronnie Kray, had managed, ninja-like, to scale the fence of the pen and break through the hedges to reach Claudette's girls. As always, we had to stop for coffee first and, because it was a chilly morning, Claudette added a generous glug of dark rum and a sugar cube. We practically ran around the garden after that and easily caught the amorous bird.

For most of that week the wind whooshed through the valley, howling dramatically around the house. The chickens hated it and hid in the coop, all except for Reggie and Ronnie Kray. They ran about flapping their wings and screeching. The chickens all live pretty much happily together, hopping from pen to pen, though Roger Moore rules his roost with a sharp beak and is definitely not keen on sharing the ladies. Not everyone agrees with this. Reggie once fell head over heels for Annette, a fluffy and rather ancient miniature coquette, and, tempted by his youthful good looks, she squeezed through the wire fence of the pen, he hopped over the top and together they eloped into the garden where they conducted their tête-à-tête away from Roger Moore's beady eyes. Each night she returned to the pen and joined the rest of the gang. Reggie and Ronnie sleep in a tree overlooking her pen, and Reggie would make gooey eyes at his true love from his perch.

But Annette eventually tired of her young lover, leaving Reggie heartbroken. Every day he hopped over the fence, calling to her, cooing, cajoling and cock-a-doodle-dooing. The hard-hearted Annette was unmoved and Reggie became a lonely cockerel.

So, we created a new pen for Reggie and bought some more chickens from the garden centre, even though I had just assured our vet that I had no intention of taking on any more animals. And as I explained to Jean-Claude, who thought we were preposterous to pander to the whims of a bird, they say money can't buy love – but in this case, they're wrong. He just raised his bushy eyebrows and shook his head.

We stuck the new girls – Zsa Zsa Gabor, Elizabeth Taylor, Doris Day and Rita Hayworth – in a coop with Reggie before nightfall. In the morning I got up early to let them out. The girls were wary: it was their first time outside of a cage. Reggie looked a bit confused by the whole thing initially, but then it was Reggie-steady-go – he did a little happy dance and the rest of the chickens and ducks welcomed the newbies with an almighty orchestra of clucks, quacks and cackling.

We'd been to the vets twice that week. The first time we went, we made him raise his eyebrows even higher than usual when we asked if there was anything we could do to help a lopsided chirping chick that we'd named Wonky Neck. He said we're 'too soft', which I think is polite French for soft in the head. The vet treats all the animals that cross our path – a motley lot, deaf, one-eyed, sick, sad and starving.

'You need to stop taking in every stray animal that comes your way. Your neighbours will tie their old farm stock to your gate one of these days.'

The second visit was with Marie-Antoinette, a very pretty cat with long, fluffy grey hair and the greenest of eyes. Completely deaf and very nervous, she once belonged to neighbours who lived in our road. They had moved to a house over 15 kilometres away and left the poor cat behind. It took me a good few months of feeding her and blinking my eyes slowly at her (I read somewhere that this is cat for 'I trust you', though Mark tells me I look just a little bit crazy when I'm doing it) to gain her confidence. Eventually, the blinking paid off and Marie-Antoinette allowed herself to be picked up and transported to the vet. We get all our cats neutered as there are already more than enough of them living in barns and wild in the woods in these parts.

'We'd like you to make sure she can't have any more babies,' I'd said to the vet.

'Your will is done. She is a he, and he has been neutered.'

You'd think we'd be able to spot the difference by now, wouldn't you? The vet told us kindly that in fact it's a mistake that plenty of people make.

If you were to ask me to list the main traits of the people in this area, the *paysans* and the ordinary country people – and that is not an insult, to be a *paysan* is not to be a peasant but to be someone who is connected to the land; it's considered something to be proud of and farming folk are held in high esteem here – I would say they are kind and generous-natured like our vet. And they all love a party.

As we headed towards spring, the days got longer and less damp. This is the time when the festival season starts and in France just about anything can be celebrated – all it takes is a big dose of passion and an audience willing to appreciate it. There are carnivals of all sorts, from the noisy and authentic in Dunkirk to the glitzy Nice Carnival, one of the most uplifting, soul-inspiring winter fêtes I've ever been to. First off, it's normally warm and sunny, with bright blue skies that chase the winter blues away and make you feel as if spring has arrived early, even though the event usually takes place in February or March. But it's the sheer passion for dance and music, the witty and fabulous figures in the parade, and the throwing of bucketloads of confetti all over each other in pure joy which creates a sort of comradeship that makes this such a memorable event. Just up the road in Menton at around the same time, the *Fête du citron* uses an estimated 150,000 kilograms of oranges and lemons in the creation of colourful and flamboyant sculptures up to 10 metres high for an annual event in honour of the fruit that grows so prolifically in the area.

But not all festivals are so glamorous. For example, the grand and illustrious International Agricultural Show which is held annually in Paris. It attracts key players from the agricultural industry, not only from France but from around the world, to showcase livestock, vegetables, crops and plants. It also features those who are very passionate about agricultural things that are a little more unusual. For instance, people who imitate pigs – and I'm not telling porkies here. There is a *Cri de cochon* – pig-squealing – contest held each year. Its human competitors imitate amorous pigs, suckling pigs and pigs on their way to pig heaven. Of course, the contestants are also dressed for the occasion, complete with ears, tail and teats.

But there can only be one winner and often it is a man called Noël Jamet, a native of Normandy, whose impressions of a breastfeeding pig, complete with small toy piglets, are legendary: so much so that he is available for squealing at weddings, anniversaries and birthdays.

The most renowned events are about food – the chickpea festival of Saint-Maximin-la-Sainte-Baume in Provence, the black pudding (or blood sausage) fair of Mortagne-au-Perche in Normandy and the *Fête de la fraise* in Beaulieu-sur-Dordogne, where there's a celebration of strawberries and all the towns' bakers get together to create the world's biggest strawberry tart: a whopping 8 metres in diameter containing up to 800 kilograms of fruit!

Whatever the weather, wherever you are in France, the French will always find an excuse for a party.

CHAPTER 11

Toujours la France!

'I'VE COME TO tell you I'm putting up a new fence at the bottom of your garden this afternoon.'

Finding Thierry the farmer standing at the front door was the first surprise of the day. We've only ever seen him a handful of times outside of his trusty and brightly coloured green-and-yellow John Deere tractor in the whole time we've had a house here. When we first moved in, he and the tractor came to our rescue a couple of times. Once, when our septic tank blew up, it was Thierry who drove into the garden dragging a cylinder-shaped tank to clear away the mess. And another time he helped rid us of a coal oven that had been left in the house by a previous owner. Not a trendy coal oven, you understand – it was at least fifty years old, caked with soot inside, the white enamel was chipped, and the metal pipe that would have pumped out the smoke from the back of it through the wall and into the garden was filled with 1970s newspapers to stop the cold and prevent critters from coming in and living inside it. Thierry 'collects' things. His large barns are full of broken furniture and appliances of all types, and he even has piles of local flint stone that he's dug out of the fields. 'You never know when it might come in handy,' he says.

Thierry has a reputation for being thrifty. His wife Mathilde says that he would sooner move to Paris than spend money on fripperies, and that's never going to happen. No one from this village has ever moved to Paris.

The second surprise was discovering that Thierry was going to put up a new fence, when for months he had been piling up bits of trees, old bed frames, random pieces of metal and broken chairs from his barn collection against the ramshackle fence between our garden and the field he rents from Claudette for his cows. He'd accidentally destroyed the fence while cutting trees around the perimeter of the field – five years ago. We weren't worried about it; the chickens and ducks had never made any attempt to get out over the top. They know which side their bread is buttered on.

And the third surprise was that he asked if he could come and retrieve his cow from our garden.

'Yes, you see, one of my cows, not a very big one, but big enough, it's managed to break through the fence. Old Man Leroy's donkey got into the field and it spooked the herd. Anyway, there's only one cow in your garden at the moment, but there's a whole load of them out there in the field, so I think it would be good if we went and dealt with it right now in case they all decide to come visiting ...'

I was just thinking about exactly how we were going to deal with it, when Jean-Claude appeared at the back of the house and stuck his head through the door.

'I was planting up some potatoes in Claudette's garden and I've just seen a cow in your garden. It's at the end of one of your duck pens.'

We have three duck pens. Rocky, Mel Gibson and Steven Seagal are in one pen where they have learned to live together, though Rocky requires his food to be served away from the other two who are more belligerent and tend to bully him; in the middle pen, Chuck Norris and Bruce Willis spend most of the time patrolling the fence and rucking from a distance with their duck neighbours; and occupying the last pen is Tony Manero, who is calm when he is alone or with the chickens, but will fight with any duck that has the misfortune to cross his path.

'It's one of Thierry's cows,' I replied. 'Apparently it's frightened of donkeys, so he's come round to sort it out.'

'He's going to need some help,' said Jean-Claude, arching one bushy eyebrow. 'Cows can be buggers to deal with – I'd rather catch an elephant. It's just as well I came.'

I could hear Thierry muttering from inside the kitchen. He and Jean-Claude would describe themselves as *copains* (mates), but they do like to compete with each other.

The four of us made our way down to the bottom of the garden which at first glance looked fairly normal.

It features a substantial area of molehill–ridden lawn dotted with trees of all kinds, including oak, quince, magnolia, pine, hazel and ornamental cherry. There's also a large metal gazebo with tables and chairs in the middle overlooking the hills that surround the village, two sizeable greenhouses running along the fence between our garden and Claudette's, and at the bottom is a small orchard of plum, cherry, apple and pear trees. But when we were halfway down the garden, just as we passed a bunch of spreading sumac trees, we could see an enormous cow in Tony Manero's pen. It was white with patches of black, blinking at us through long eyelashes – rather docilely, I thought. It seemed oblivious to the screeching chickens and ducks, and I am sure it must have been confused, having made the effort to get there, to discover that the grass had been annihilated: the chickens had long since taken care of anything that grew there and tasted good.

'*Merde*, it really is an elephant, *oh là là … là là*,' said Jean-Claude, sighing deeply.

Behind the fence, a gang of fifteen or so cows stood placid and curious, craning their necks to look at their brave friend, but not coming through the gaping hole. They were possibly put off by seeing the boss on the other side or perhaps unnerved by the donkey, which was braying at the top of its voice and charging around almost gleefully, leaping and kicking its legs out.

'Right,' said Thierry authoritatively, 'cow psychology

basics. We'll never get this sorted out with that bloody donkey out there. We must go and take it back to Old Man Leroy. Jean-Claude and I will do it, as we are the experienced farmers, and then we will come straight back. If you could just stay here and keep an eye on the cow; she's not likely to push any more fences down and get in your garden.'

I wasn't sure I believed that, but had little choice since they had already let themselves into the pen. Then they headed off into the field through the gap, observed by the placid cow. The herd ran away from them and formed a tight-knit group over on the other side of the field, and we all watched as the two ageing donkey-hunters ran about, treading in great dollops of cow poo, waving their arms wildly, bickering and telling each other what to do, as they tried to drive the ass into a corner where they could tie a rope round its neck and lead it out. They eventually managed to do so, giving us a thumbs-up and grinning, breathlessly triumphant after their exertions.

The escaped cow, meanwhile, wandered towards the hole in the fence, no doubt having realized that the grass is not always greener. It stepped back into the field and walked over to its friends without looking back.

Using a bit of old plastic roofing from behind the greenhouse, we dragged it across the hole and secured it with some wire. 'It'll hold until Thierry mends it,' Mark assured me.

By the time Jean-Claude and Thierry had stopped to

chat to Old Man Leroy, then walked back past the field, out into the alley and round to our house having found themselves unable to get back through the garden now we'd blocked up the fence, Mark and I were relaxing outdoors with Mathilde, who had come looking for her husband as he'd been gone so long.

'Look out, here come Clint Eastwood and John Wayne,' said Mathilde, smirking as the pair approached. After a couple of celebratory beers with everyone, it was time for Thierry to take the cows home for milking. The fence was repaired properly the next day.

'Glad to be of service,' said Jean-Claude after Thierry and Mathilde had left, as usual hogging the glory. 'Before I go, I've got a favour to ask. Remember I told you that I was having a knee operation and you said you'd help me with the New People's horses? Well, the operation is the day after tomorrow. Can you go to their house and feed the horses for me in the mornings for a few days and just pop in on them in the evenings to make sure everything's okay? I'll let you know when I'm back in action.'

Two mornings later, we arrived at the house of the New People as arranged, and were about to let ourselves in through the side gate as Jean-Claude had instructed, when a woman leaned out of a window on the ground floor. It was Mrs New Person. She told us that she and her husband had arranged to work from home and look after the horses while Jean-Claude was recuperating so that he, and we, wouldn't have to worry. She invited us in for coffee and said that she, real name Vanessa, and her husband Benoît, would be around for the next few days, after which time they hoped their horse helper would be able to return. They were glad of the chance to spend more time here, as they'd been so busy with work that they hadn't had the opportunity to really get to know the area that well.

'Why don't you join us for aperitifs next Friday?' asked Mark. 'We meet up with Jean-Claude and Bernadette once a month and it's our turn to host that week. Ours is the house with the blue shutters to the side of the town hall, opposite the house of the always-barking Labradoodle and next door to Claudette – the only house in the village with a slate roof.'

As Mark said this, the thought popped into my head that he was sounding like a local, describing where we live instead of giving a street number, name and postcode. It's how it's done here, keeping things simple.

Later that week we sat in Arnaud's bar, having stopped off on our way home from collecting a bale of hay for a major spring clean of the chicken coops, and it occurred to me that if we weren't both totally native then we must be pretty close to it.

'What if ...' began Monsieur Lafont, who was sitting at the table in the centre of the bar, addressing Mark and I, Monsieur Martinez and Nanette the local hairdresser (who had just finished work in her salon, a converted garage at the side of her house that is large enough for just two customers and, unless you want the same short, feathery haircut as everyone else in the village, is to be avoided at all costs).

'What if we had our own local Olympics? All this talk on the telly of Paris 2024 and the Olympics has got me pondering. I'm not talking about gymnastics or ice skating or anything like that, though last week I did see Monique the barmaid walking her dog' – he looked around to make sure she hadn't arrived for work yet with the yappy, unfriendly Petit Chou whom everyone detests – 'and she slid on a patch of ice outside the boulangerie and wibbled and wobbled all over the place, but managed to stay up and keep hold of the dog and her baguette, so I reckon she'd be in with a chance on the skating rink. But I was thinking we could come up with some events based on what we know best, you know, country skills …'

The general hum of conversation in the room suddenly went quiet. Arnaud was standing behind the zinc-covered counter, slowly drying a glass with a cloth, twisting it round and round, a thoughtful look on his face.

Monsieur Martinez was occupying his usual place at a corner table. 'I like it. You know, I think you might be on to something there. Arnaud, let's see how fast you can pour me another glass of that La Goudale Ambrée beer,' he said, chortling.

Monsieur Lafont emitted an unimpressed '*Pfff*' and turned away from Monsieur Martinez to look at me and Mark. 'I was thinking tractor-racing, guess the weight of the bull, animal noise impressions … What do you think, *les Anglais*?' he asked.

'How about an egg-throwing contest?' I suggested, not thinking the idea of rustic Olympics remotely odd.

Monsieur Dubarre, a long time regular, was sitting on a stool at the bar with Beau, Arnaud's huge dog, asleep at his feet. For several years he'd been trying to teach Beau to bark at the word 'president', and had claimed some success as the dog barks whenever he comes into the bar in anticipation of getting a treat, and Monsieur Dubarre always says to him: '*Bonjour Monsieur le Président.*'

He put down the newspaper he'd been reading and proposed hay-bale rolling. 'Or what about a cheese-eating contest? I'd be pretty good at that one.'

Monsieur Lafont said it would be impossible as there are too many champions of this sport already.

'Boules,' said Mark.

'*Pardon?*' said Monsieur Dubarre

'Boules! It should be an Olympic sport.'

Well, that got him brownie points straight away, despite it not being a country skill. For decades, the French have been attempting to get boules on the Olympic events list but alas, even for Paris 2024 it was turned down by the International Olympic Committee.

My neighbours are keen on boules but not as much

as in some parts of France, where there has recently been mention of *bouliganisme*, where some teams have been getting carried away and acting like hooligans in their efforts to win village boules competitions by intimidating umpires and even throwing a few punches. There's nothing like that round here, I can tell you.

Jean-Claude got his pal Denis to teach us the rules after we helped him to build a boules pitch on the village green. He doesn't play himself, but he loves to watch a game with a glass of pastis of an evening. It is, he says, the perfect way to relax: sitting under the oak tree, listening to the satisfying click–clack of metal balls thwacking together, the under-the-breath muttering of those who don't hit home, the triumphant '*oulà*' of those who do …

Boules is the most popular ball game in France and is played nationally by approximately 20 million people. It's fairly simple but it requires skill and concentration. Players throw a heavy ball (usually made of steel and marked with different patterns to help you recognize your balls from those of other players) at a *cochonnet*, which means 'piglet' in French, but in this case refers to a small wooden ball. The basic aim of the game is very simple: competitors, either individually or in two teams of two (*doublettes*) or three (*triplettes*), must toss their balls as close to the *cochonnet* as possible.

Denis, nicknamed Le Vieux since he has been playing boules for longer than anyone can remember – 'Longer than anyone has been alive,' cackled Jean-Claude when he introduced us – is known to be one of the best players in the valleys, a several-times local champion. It was impossible to guess his age. His ruddy face was creased and wrinkled, white eyebrows showed beneath a cap he never removed, and he was slightly bent over at all times. Regardless, he put us through our paces.

'Loosen up, swing your arms, lift your knees up, twist.' We were stood at the edge of the pitch. The post lady went by in her little yellow van, then reversed. She got out and brought our post over.

'Don't interrupt them,' said Le Vieux. 'These *Anglais* need to concentrate, they're as green as grass at this game.'

The lesson lasted an hour and mainly involved us being shouted at: 'Right, stand in that circle, point your right foot where you want your ball to go, hold it properly like I showed you, pull your arm back and flip that ball. Don't hide your light under a bushel, shine it in the opposition's eyes!'

In boules, you're allowed – in fact, you're positively encouraged – to interfere with your opponent's balls, knocking them further away from the *cochonnet* if you can. There's no such thing as letting a person win for friendship's sake. You need to go all out to win – both the game and the admiration of your French friends. Finally, Le Vieux announced he was satisfied that we could stand up to scrutiny in a game of boules.

It was agreed by all in the bar that when the time

came, a grand boules match instead of a series of games was the perfect way to join in the spirit of the Olympic Games from our rural corner of northern France.

The following week brought a special day for us. It was the sixteenth anniversary of the day that we signed the purchase papers for our old farmhouse. It's a date we cherish. It was also the day we had invited the New People over for aperitifs. I had mentioned it to Jean-Claude when I went to check on his recuperation a few days earlier.

'I'm doing well,' he said. 'I'll be back to normal in a day or so, but why don't you come to us instead for aperitifs? It'll save my knees going up and down the hill. I'll let the New People know. Come at seven o'clock.'

On the day of the rendezvous, we walked down the hill to Jean-Claude's house an hour before dusk and fifteen minutes late, the aroma of a nearby barbecue filling the air.

'Cor, that smells good,' said Mark, sniffing deeply. 'I reckon they're cooking Dhalleine's Basque sausages. It's making me really hungry.'

It takes just two minutes to reach Jean-Claude's house from ours, and the garage door was wide open. Bernadette was standing outside and beckoned us in. 'You're late,' she laughed, 'proper French now.'

We followed her into the back garden where, to our surprise, we discovered a crowd of people. Claudette was sitting in a deckchair with a blanket on her lap and

Petit Frère was standing before a smoking barbecue, the obvious source of the enticing aromas, wielding a pair of tongs and swigging from a bottle of beer. Also in attendance were the Parisians, Monsieur and Madame Rohart, Constance and Guillaume, Madame Bernadette, the Claudes – the father and son of the same name who live at opposite ends of the village – and the New People, Vanessa and Benoît. Even Thierry and Mathilde, who rarely go to evening events as they have to get up so early in the morning to deal with the cows, had made it.

'You're late,' said Jean-Claude. 'We told everyone to be here for six-thirty thinking you'd arrive on time and here you are, late.'

'*Bah*, they're proper local now!' Petit Frère grinned.

There were kisses all round, someone thrust a glass of red wine into my hand and gave Mark some beer. Everyone was talking, and Petit Frère called out for us to come and get a long, fat, perfectly barbecued sausage, and to help ourselves to buttered potatoes and bread from the kitchen. We stood around chatting and drinking under the darkening sky, batting away moths lured by the lamps that Bernadette had lit.

'These sausages are absolutely delicious,' remarked Vanessa. 'I must ask Petit Frère where he got them from.'

'It has to be Dhalleine's,' said Mark.

'But which ones?' asked Petit Frère, who had overheard the conversation as he was wandered past on his way to get another beer from the kitchen.

'Basque.'

Petit Frère grinned and nodded. He came back with his drink and a plate of cheese.

'Where'd this come from then?' he asked, indicating the dairy items he was carrying.

'Caseus, Montreuil-sur-Mer, except for the goats' cheese – that's from the Goat Lady at Hesmond,' I answered without hesitation. I couldn't tell from looking at the cheese, but everyone knows that Caseus is the best fromagerie in the area and that Valérie makes the best goats' cheese in France at her little farm down the road.

'Correct again,' said Petit Frère.

Vanessa asked where she should go for the best bread, cakes, wines and vegetables.

'There are so many great bread and cake shops everywhere, but rue de Metz in Le Touquet has some of the best. And Pâtisserie Grémont at Montreuil-sur-Mer. And, of course, Bread Man,' Mark replied.

'Oliviers at Montreuil-sur-Mer for wine or the Caves du Vieux Chai at Fressin,' I said. 'Depends on the day of the week for markets to get your vegetables, but Saint-Omer on a Saturday morning is one of the best in France.'

Our French friends nodded in agreement as they listened. And I realized in that instant that we had really become locals, no longer *les étrangers*, the strangers. We were giving advice, we were now part of the village.

Jean-Claude handed out sparkling wine to everyone and then clinked a fork against his glass to still all the conversations.

'Today is officially the *Fête des voisins* [Neighbours' Day] and we're all really happy to meet the new people in the village, Vanessa and Benoît. But it's also the anniversary of the day that Mark and Janine bought their house in our little village and decided to join us here. Cheers everyone.'

We all held our glasses up and toasted each other with a heartfelt '*santé*'. I held Mark's hand and felt my eyes prick with tears as everyone clapped. I looked around at the wonderful friends we've made here in this tiny hamlet in the middle of nowhere, in this most beautiful part of the far north of France. Not a day goes by when I don't thank my lucky stars that we accidentally discovered a ramshackle hovel in a village that we'd never heard of and made our home in the place where they say people have sunshine in their hearts.

Toujours la France ...

Also by Janine Marsh

MY GOOD LIFE IN FRANCE:
IN PURSUIT OF THE RURAL DREAM
978-1-78243-732-1

MY FOUR SEASONS IN FRANCE:
A YEAR OF THE GOOD LIFE
978-1-78929-047-9

£9.99

Available in paperback and ebook formats